Educational Administration and History

In the past 40 years there have been a number of significant developments across the fields of educational administration and history. In this volume, the authors have selected a number of key issues to illustrate and trace these changes. The seven chapters by leading scholars in the field offer an analysis of contemporary educational administration, history and policy debates and how this has impacted on teachers, leaders, schools and the education sector. This book offers readers a valuable insight into continuing and contemporary debates in the field and the authors offer a refreshing interpretation of these debates. This book provides a rich analysis from a range of theoretical, methodological perspectives and highlights the extent to which these debates remain a contemporary concern.

This book was published as a special issue of the *Journal of Educational Administration and History*.

Tanya Fitzgerald is Professor of Education at Unitec Institute of Technology, Auckland, New Zealand. Tanya has an extensive publishing record on the history of women's education, gender, leadership and ethnicity, and teachers' work. As well as co-editor of the *Journal of Educational Administration and History*, Tanya is executive editor of *History of Education Review* and the *New Zealand Journal of Educational Leadership, Policy and Practice*. Her forthcoming book is a study of women professors at the University of New Zealand 1911-1961.

Helen Gunter is Professor of Education Policy, Leadership and Management in the School of Education, University of Manchester, UK. Helen's research interests focus on the history of the field, with a particular interest in knowledge production through theorising, research and practice. She has published five books and over 70 papers, and is currently co-editor of the *Journal of Educational Administration and History*.

Educational Administration and History

The state of the field

Edited by Tanya Fitzgerald and Helen Gunter

Routledge
Taylor & Francis Group
LONDON AND NEW YORK

First published 2009 by Routledge
2 Park Square, Milton Park, Abingdon, Oxon, OX14 4RN

Simultaneously published in the USA and Canada
by Routledge
270 Madison Avenue, New York, NY 10016

Routledge is an imprint of the Taylor & Francis Group, an informa business

Typeset in Times by Value Chain, India
Printed and bound in Great Britain by MPG Books Ltd. Bodmin, Cornwall

British Library Cataloguing in Publication Data
A catalogue record for this book is available from the British Library

ISBN10: 0-415-46887-6
ISBN13: 978-0-415-46887-9

CONTENTS

NOTES ON CONTRIBUTORS

Richard Bates is Professor of Education (Social and Administrative Studies) in the Faculty of Education at Deakin University. His scholarly work has been concerned with the Sociology of Education (where he contributed to the debate over the new sociology of education in Britain in the 1970s) and Educational Administration (where he contributed to the emergence of an alternative 'critical' theory during the 1980s). His work as Dean (1986–2000) drew him into debates over teacher education and his Presidency of the Victorian and Australian Councils of Deans of Education led him to contest official views regarding teacher supply and demand, and challenge the marginalisation of teacher education programmes. He is past President of the Australian Teacher Education Association, a past President of the Australian Association for Researchers in Education and a Fellow of the Australian College of Education and of the Australian Council for Educational Administration. He is currently writing about morals and markets, public education, ethics and administration, the impact of educational research, and social justice and the aesthetics of educational administration as well as global teacher education.

Scott Eacott is a lecturer in the School of Education, the University of Newcastle, Australia. He has primarily written on the strategic role of the educational leader (the focus of his doctoral work), however more recently Scott received a Teaching and Learning Fellowship through the Centre for Teaching and Learning at the University of Newcastle and is conducting a series of studies on the instructional practices of educational leadership programmes particularly in the online environment.

Tanya Fitzgerald is Professor of Education at Unitec Institute of Technology, Auckland, New Zealand. Her research interests include the history of women's higher education, academic women and the development of historical identity, teachers' work and education policy, educational biography and narrative inquiry. Her forthcoming book *Outsider or Equals: A History of Women Professors at the University of New Zealand 1911–1961* is to be published by Peter Lang. Tanya is co-editor of the *Journal of Educational Administration and History*, co-editor of *History of Education Review* and editor of the *Journal of Educational Leadership, Policy and Practice.*

Peter Gronn is Professor of Public Service, Educational Leadership and Management in the Department of Educational Studies, University of Glasgow. Previously, he was Professor in the Faculty of Education, Monash University. In two projects he is currently researching head teacher recruitment and retention, and the preparation of school leaders through coaching. He was a consultant to the Australian Council for Educational Research on the project 'Standards for School Leadership' and in 2006–7 he co-authored the Country Background Report for Australia which formed part of the OECD international project on school leadership.

Helen Gunter is Professor of Educational Policy, Leadership and Management in the School of Education, University of Manchester. She has produced over 70 publications including books and papers on leadership theory and practice. She is particularly interested in the history of the field of leadership, with a focus on knowledge production. She has recently completed an ESRC-funded project into the rise of school leadership under New Labour. Her most recent book, co-edited with Graham Butt, University of Birmingham, is about workforce reform: *Modernizing Schools: People, Learning and Organizations* (Continuum, 2007).

Pat Thomson is Professor of Education and Director of Research in the School of Education, The University of Nottingham. Her research interests include the changing work practices of headteachers; the arts, inclusive pedagogies and school change; and doctoral education. She has just recently edited *Doing Visual Research with Children and Young People* (Routledge, 2008) and is now working on two Routledge books, one on headteacher supply and retention, and another on changing schools through systematic inquiry.

Jane Wilkinson currently lectures in education at Charles Sturt University, Wagga Wagga, Australia. Her doctoral thesis examined representations of ethnically and socioeconomically diverse women leaders in the Australian media and universities. She has published in a variety of areas including praxis and educational leadership, diversity policies and their implications for women's leadership and critical feminist scholarship. She recently has been a visiting scholar at the University of Nottingham and the University of Manchester, UK.

Terry Wrigley is a senior lecturer in the Moray House School of Education, University of Edinburgh. His research interests include school development and social justice, with a particular emphasis on class. His publications include three books: *The Power to Learn* (2000), *Schools of Hope* (2003) and *Another School Is Possible* (2006).

Introduction: the state of the field of educational administration

Tanya Fitzgerald and Helen Gunter

As noted in the editorial in Volume 40, Number 1, the *Journal of Educational Administration and History* [JEAH] is in its 40th year. This occasion is therefore an opportunity to reflect not only on the journal and its contribution to the field, but the theoretical and methodological state of the field itself. With this in mind we have invited seven authors to offer a critical reflection on key issues that underpin the field. Accordingly, in the collection of papers in this book, attention is focused on the identification and critique of key concepts and issues that include headteacher's critique of and resistance to policy, the intersectionality of gender, leadership and ethnicity, ongoing issues in teacher performance management, the orthodoxies of school effectiveness research, a critical analysis of texts related to the field, and the modernisation agenda. This book concludes with an analysis of the preceding papers and their contribution to debates in and the development of the field of educational administration.

The focus that we have elected 'The state of the field of educational administration', is not accidental. The genesis of this book began with a conversation amongst a group of scholars that critical debates should continue to surface in journals such as JEAH as well as in scholarly texts. Essentially we were troubled that the term 'critical' was, at times, juxtaposed with the term 'oppositional' and this was not our collective reading of what being critical, engaging in critical dialogue and what our contribution to critical scholarship entailed. We saw an interconnection between critical reading, critical writing and critical thinking that contributed to current debates and scholarship in the field. By inference, this does not involve a rehearsal of debates but the adoption of a stance that surfaced critical questions concerning the nature and shape of knowledge, how this knowledge was being produced and by whom and the underpinning construction of this knowledge for the field. What remains problematic is that knowledge production is frequently linked with the agenda of the State as we have commented on previously.[1] It is essential that critical debates concerning knowledge production continue to occur

---

[1] See here Gunter, H.M and Fitzgerald, T. (2008) Educational administration and history: Debating the agenda, *Journal of Educational Administration & History,* 40(1): 5-20; Gunter, H.M and Fitzgerald, T. (2008) The future of leadership research? *School Leadership & Management*, (in press).

and that the insistent presence of a neo-liberal reform agenda continues to be critically evaluated, not the least because of its impact on the field and field development.

In order to publicly debate these agendas and surface our disquiet concerning the state of the field, this group of scholars collectively engaged in a connected symposium at the September 2007 British Educational Leadership Management and Administration (BELMAS) conference in Reading. The underpinning concern of the architects of this symposium was that the field of educational administration appeared to be at a point of theoretical disconnection and, accordingly, we shaped our presentations around our concerns. Each of the papers traversed some of the current debates and highlighted the extent to which knowledge production remains connected with a neo-liberal State. In order to draw together the theoretical and methodological threads of these papers, Peter Gronn acted as discussant and reflected on the extent to which the papers highlighted and extended the issues. Substantially revised and lengthened, these papers are collected together in this book.

Documenting debates

As we have indicated, this book highlights a number of contemporary policy and scholarship issues that underpin the field of educational administration. As editors of a learned journal in the field, our challenge is to ensure that a plurality of voices is encouraged and that wider debate about purposes and practices in the field is surfaced. The authors featured in this book, have not only responded to this challenge but have offered their own nuanced understandings of these contemporary issues. What is refreshing, we believe, is that the authors have not simply rehearsed debates but offered their own critical stance that challenges the field itself. How can the field be renewed and re-invigorated with robust debate?

The first contribution by Pat Thomson interrogates the extent to which headteachers deal with escalating policy demands and considers how their agency fosters a level of resistance. In a direct theoretical and empirical challenge to the field, the author challenges headteachers (as professionals) and academics (as scholars) to consider how collective action might 'speak back' to policy regimes that are deeply inequitable. Importantly, Thomson raises questions concerning headteachers' voices and the potential for their critical *and* collective voice to take up multiple subject positions and re-frame the research agenda. Importantly, there is a call from the author for the field to consider ways in which headteachers and headteacher associations might contribute to knowledge production in the field that can offer a rich perspective.

In similar ways, Jane Wilkinson, in the second paper, extends the call for multiple voices and highlights the diversity of possibilities for the field if it is 'opened-up' to the inclusion of critical, Black, feminist and Indigenous perspectives. Notably, Wilkinson takes seriously recent calls for research and theorising to include in more explicit ways notions of diversity and leadership in ways that are conceptually rich, socially just, educationally transformative, as well as providing critically reflexive possibilities. As part of her own reflexive turn, the author examines the interplay of her own biography and scholarship in the field and proposes that serious questions concerning power and knowledge production should be more insistently raised. Wilkinson concludes by suggesting that active intervention is required if genuinely productive, democratic and socially inclusive ways of leading are to be realised and actioned.

In her analysis of teacher performance management, Tanya Fitzgerald highlights ways in which the continuing lack of trust in teachers has underpinned the development and implementation of policy and associated practices. Performance management, as a policy solution to the 'problem' of teachers, is, according to the author, predicated on the flawed assumption that the intervention of the State and its agencies is required to ensure that teachers' work is aligned with organisational objectives. Accordingly, the shift in teacher accountability from the profession to the State has, in effect, served to de-professionalise teaching and teachers' work.

The historical construct and emergence of school improvement is examined by Terry Wrigley. Arguing that the concept of improvement is intrinsically ideological, the author argues that the significant and explicit paradigm change that occurred in the early 1990s, resulted in a managerialist and reductionist approach to improving schools that exacerbated poverty and inequities rather than alleviated, or mediated, its effects. One of the key features of Wrigley's paper is that he overviews the emergence in England of school improvement and school effectiveness studies and therefore reminds readers of the long-term consequences of these paradigms.

Richard Bates and Scott Eacott offer a challenge to those working in the field of higher education. That is, they challenge field members to consider the texts that are in use, those that are discarded and the extent to which these texts can be used to formulate the knowledge that is taught, reinforced, received and, at times, regurgitated. Drawing on evidence from the Australian context, the authors question the 'local', 'global' and 'international' and via their highly nuanced study of educational administration programmes in Australia, conclude that there is a focus on the academic (as opposed to the technical and operational) but that there is a steady albeit worrying decline in numbers of Australian studies and authors being used. Central to their analysis are questions about how texts are used (or mis-used), reflected on or deflected in current and contemporary debates. Essentially Bates and Eacott ask - in what ways might the field be complicit, intended or otherwise, in its own demise by decisions made as to which texts are 'worthy' and which ones are to be discarded? How might the field be 'read' if texts are used as evidence of what 'counts'?

The penultimate contribution by Helen Gunter provides a theoretical backdrop for this book. The author's examination of modernisation and Barber's policy implementation strategies is a refreshing account of history-making and history-writing as a deeply complex and contested process. Arguably too, the 'deliverology' and its consequences that Gunter highlights have similarly surfaced in the work of Thomson, Fitzgerald, and Wrigley. In her call for ongoing dialogue about the nature of the field and what scholarship is in practice, Gunter highlights the central concerns that led to the BELMAS seminar and this collection of papers. The passionate plea for field members to engage in debate and dialogue and position themselves as central to the development of the field is a challenge that requires response.

Drawing this all together, Peter Gronn has used the metaphorical 'turn' of Hamlet and the state of Denmark to not only reflect and comment on the papers in this book but also to contribute his own critical ideas to how the field, the 'kingdom', has developed and the challenges it continues to face. This is a paper that can well preface as well as summarise the contributions and we would like to suggest can and should act as a catalyst for continuing these critical debates.

Headteacher critique and resistance: a challenge for policy, and for leadership/management scholars

Pat Thomson

Educational administration scholars are concerned to examine leadership/management in specific policy contexts. In the UK, as in other parts of the world, investigations have focused on how headteachers deal with highly centralised and rapidly churning policy agendas, audit and inspection regimes, media and markets, and escalating expectations about student attainment, engagement and retention.[1] Some have pursued the specific circumstances of headteachers in the most challenging circumstances.[2]

Implicitly or explicitly, all of these studies address the structural constraints that frame and delimit headteacher autonomy, freedom, agency and power. Many describe headteacher *mediation* of structural imposts. Day and colleagues, for example suggest that heads can and do make decisions about what happens in their school, selectively following and ignoring what they deem appropriate.[3] Thrupp and Wilmott have dubbed this analysis a

---

[1]For example, Tony Bush, Les Bell, Ray Bolam, Ron Glatter, and Peter Ribbins, *Educational Management: Redefining Theory, Policy and Practice* (London: Paul Chapman Publishing, 1999); and Peter Earley, ed., *School Improvement After Inspection? School and LEA Responses* (London: Paul Chapman Publishing, 1998).

[2]For example, Mel Ainscow and Mel West, eds., *Improving Urban Schools. Leadership and Collaboration* (Buckingham, UK: Open University Press, 2006); Alma Harris, Sue James, Judith Gunraj, Paul Clarke, and Belinda Harris, *Improving Schools in Exceptionally Challenging Circumstances. Tales from the Frontline* (London: Continuum, 2006); John Macbeath, John Gray, Jane Cullen, David Frost, Susan Steward, and Sue Swaffield, *Schools on the Edge. Responding to Challenging Circumstances* (London: Paul Chapman Publishing, 2007).

[3]Chris Day, Alma Harris, Mark Hadfield, Harry Tolley, and John Beresford, *Leading Schools in Times of Change* (Buckingham, UK: Open University Press, 2000).

'textual apology', an academic cover-up of the multiple accommodations that heads make to audit and performance regimes.[4] Thrupp argues that there is no scholarly investigation of headteacher critique of or resistance to managerialist policy[5] – but there ought to be.

In this article I focus on the questions that Thrupp raises. I argue that if the field is to take critique and resistance seriously it will need to: interrogate and test out the limits of the proposition through empirical example; consider instances where it does appear to occur; and move beyond a focus on individual headteachers to take seriously their collective professional organisations.

I begin with a brief discussion of the scholarly 'problem' of agency, critique and resistance.

What can headteachers do?

Scholars have long struggled to understand the organisation, production, reproduction and transformation of social life. Disciplines such as philosophy, sociology and anthropology have endeavoured to get beyond dualistic inside–outside explanations of social practice. Philosophers highlight the role of language, knowledge and the historical/cultural specificities of understanding.[6] Social scientists focus on structure/agency: if humans do not have the free will to do exactly what they want, and if their actions are not completely determined by history, language, the practices of class, race, gender and so on, as well as by social conventions and rules, then how is individual and collective agency to be theorised.[7] Cultural theorists move beyond notions of structure to consider questions of interaction and discourse,[8] while students of science and technology focus on understanding actions and actors[9] and activity.[10] Much of this scholarship has a decided 'practice' turn and not only assumes that social practice is embodied, but also that it operates within specific fields, and at specific times and scales.[11]

---

[4]Martin Thrupp and Robert Wilmott, *Educational Management in Managerialist Times: Beyond the Textual Apologists* (Buckingham, UK: Open University Press, 2003).

[5]Martin Thrupp, *School Improvement: An Unofficial Approach* (London: Continuum, 2005).

[6]For example, Ludwig Wittgenstein, *Philosophical Investigations* (Oxford: Basil Blackwell, 1976).

[7]For example, Pierre Bourdieu on habitus in *The Logic of Practice* (Stanford, CA: Stanford University Press, 1990); Anthony Giddens on structuration in *Central Problems in Social Theory* (Berkeley: University of California Press, 1979); and Dorothy Smith on the relations of ruling in *The Everyday World as Problematic. A Feminist Sociology* (Boston: Northeastern University Press, 1987).

[8]For example, Michel Foucault, *The Archeology of Knowledge* (Routledge: London, 1972); Jean Francois Lyotard, *The Postmodern Condition: A Report on Knowledge* (Minneapolis: University of Minnesota Press, 1984).

[9]For example, Bruno Latour, *Science in Action. How to Follow Scientists and Engineers through Society* (Cambridge, MA: Harvard University Press, 1987).

[10]Lev Vygotsky, *Mind in Society: The Development of Higher Psychological Processes* (Cambridge, MA: Harvard University Press, 1978), and post-Vygotskian scholars.

[11]Theodore Schatzki, Karin Knorr Cetina, and Eike Von Savigny, eds., *The Practice Turn in Contemporary Theory* (London: Routledge, 2001).

Very little of this corpus of academic work has influenced the field of leadership/management.[12] While the how-to-do-it books assume that headteachers can do as they wish, the how-it-is books narrowly focus on the external constraints of education policy, rather than taking up the approaches used by policy sociologists, for example, policy as a matter of text/discourse[13] or as context/text and effect.[14]

My first contention is that this narrow academic engagement – with the traditions of the social sciences by many in the leadership/management field – limits the kinds of questions that are asked, the studies that are mounted, and the explanations that are offered. I indicate in this article that a more expansive theoretical repertoire supports the investigation of the question of critique and resistance.

Social sciences approaches to resistance

The responses headteachers make to policy can be conceived of as a simple duality – resistance or compliance. Resistance can be seen as an active choice, arising from a critical rejection of government policy, whereas compliance might be the result of:

- coercion – to resist would be to bring about harsh consequences;
- corruption – the person has either been chosen to be, or has developed views and values congruent with, policy directions;
- cowardice – the person lacks the courage to do what is right;
- self-interest – the person puts their own needs (for example, salary and security) above that of others (staff and students).

The latter three interpretations are potentially offensive to those who conform, and are the kinds of conclusions that derive from an individualised 'free will' approach to understanding headteacher action. A social scientific analysis that allows movement beyond individualised insult to understanding and explanation[15] needs to take up the idea of the discursive positioning of headteachers, and/or interrogate their habitus and their 'stakes' in the field,[16] in order to show what actions are possible in specific circumstances.

Postcolonial scholars suggest that compliance is a complex idea. It might be the result of *emulation* – taking actions to meet expectations – or *simulation* – actions which appear

---

[12]There are of course significant exceptions and some of this work is represented in this special issue. See some US counterparts in Fenwick English, ed., *The SAGE Handbook of Educational Leadership. Advances in Theory, Research and Practice* (Thousand Oaks, CA: Sage, 2003). One theory that has been taken up with enthusiasm is Wenger's version of activity theory, communities of practice (Etienne Wenger, *Communities of Practice. Learning, Meaning and Identity*, Cambridge, MA: Cambridge University Press, 1998). A piece of work waiting to be undertaken is a deconstruction of the official policy discourse of networking and its mobilization of Wenger.

[13]Stephen Ball, 'What is Policy? Texts, Trajectories and Toolboxes', *Discourse* 13, no. 2 (1993): 3–11.

[14]Sandra Taylor, 'Critical Policy Analysis: Exploring Contexts, Texts and Consequences', *Discourse* 23, no. 13 (1997): 23–35.

[15]Pierre Bourdieu, *On Television* (New York: The New Press, 1996).

[16]See Australian scholars on leadership habitus: Jill Blackmore and Judyth Sachs, *Performing and Reforming Leaders: Gender, Educational Restructuring and Organisational Change* (New York: State University of New York Press, 2007); Bob Lingard, Pam Christie, Deborah Hayes, and Martin Mills, *Leading Learning: Making Hope Practical in Schools* (Buckingham, UK: Open University Press, 2003).

to meet expectations.[17] And simulation might be an act of camouflage, the result of an image management exercise which aims to disguise from an external gaze what is actually happening. Equally it might contain elements of satire and mimicry. Either way, from this perspective, apparent compliance can be seen as more than simple obedience and as possibly rather more tactical and strategic than might be imagined at a superficial glance. Furthermore, following this line of analysis, no matter how constrained, compliance (like resistance) is also an act of agency: the person chooses what to do in the light of how they see the expected and desired results of their actions. But what are considered valid choices are not free floating, but are discursive; that is they are the product of specific cultural and historical conventions and 'truths'. And what is possible is delimited by context, that is, the specific conjunction of histories, geographies, economics, cultures and teleologies, as well as by any specific policy agenda. It is important to note that this is only one approach to the question of compliance. Lyotard's[18] theories of performativity would not discriminate between simulation and emulation in this way at this time: both would be taken as a 'fabrication' whose accomplishment profoundly limits time and space for resistance.[19]

Resistance too is a very vexed notion, with varying interpretations in social science scholarship.[20] Some take it to mean actions in opposition to policy (this might be called overt resistance), while others include actions that are intended to shift policy (these might be seen as reforming activities, some of which occur within quite rigid bureaucratic constraints) and actions that are critical of policy (such as speaking out). There is no space to pursue the complexities of these arguments here, but they serve to demonstrate the theoretical resources that are potentially available to the leadership/management field to pose questions and/or to theorise statistical or thematised findings.

Is resistance actually happening?

My second contention concurs with Thrupp's, namely that theorisations of critique, resistance and compliance need to be developed through empirical example.

Savvy heads always take care of bureaucracy, doing just enough of what is required to maintain good relations and minimise interference.[21] However identities and practices shift as they do so within policy and wider context changes, cf. Alexiadou's study of further education managers and their pragmatic responsiveness to, proactive acceptance of, or entrepreneurial engagement with new managerialism.[22] Educational leader/managers also exhibit characteristics of Casey's 'colluded self' with its marginalisation of professional dispositions.[23] Because doing what is required (be it emulation or simulation or mediation)

---

[17]See Homi Bhabha, 'Of Mimicry and Man: The Ambivalence of Colonial Discourse', *October* 28 (1984): 125–33.
[18]Lyotard, *The Postmodern Condition*.
[19]Stephen Ball, 'The Teacher's Soul and the Terrors of Performativity', *Journal of Education Policy* 18, no. 2 (2003): 215–28.
[20]Compare Michel de Certeau, *The Practice of Everyday Life* (Los Angeles: University of California Press, 1988); Steve Pile and Michael Keith, eds., *Geographies of Resistance* (London: Routledge, 1997) and Paul Willis, *Learning to Labour. How Working Class Kids Get Working Class Jobs* (London: Saxon House, 1977).
[21]Martin Haberman, *Star Principals: Serving Children in Poverty* (Indianapolis, IN: Kappa Delta Pi, 1999).
[22]Nafsika Alexiadou, 'Management Identities in Transition: A Case Study from Further Education', *The Sociological Review* 49, no. 3 (2001): 411–35.
[23]Catherine Casey, *Work, Self and Society. After Industrialism* (London: Routledge, 1995).

is not a neutral activity, the 'self' shifts in order to align itself with organisational goals and conventions and to manage contradictions and ambiguities.[24]

Here I examine two instances to illustrate the importance of empirical investigation: the first is of headteacher refusal to implement policy, and the second of headteacher critique. These are not intended to be definitive examples but rather illustrations that suggest that many such examples are needed in order for the field to understand headteachers' oppositions to policy.

Simulating consent

Smyth and Dow argue that headteachers are not above a little simulation which allows them to make local adjustments to policy without their schools suffering the negative effects of systemic surveillance.[25] In my own research data many heads talk of selectively rejecting some changes while acceding to those that they judge relevant.[26] The majority suggest that they actively decide what to do and when and are resentful of any suggestion that they simply do as they are told.

In one interview a headteacher reported a 'mock inspection' in order to uncover the things that an Office for Standards in Education (OfSTED) inspection might highlight. This information allowed her to then quickly initiate a series of 'cover-up' actions for those things that were amenable to such transformation. In another case a headteacher outlined his belief that not only OfSTED but also researchers must be managed through a series of carefully staged events and steerage away from any areas of weakness. On yet another occasion a head, a self-styled 'fixer' who serially went into schools deemed 'failing'[27], pointed to the kinds of short-term strategies that could be used to raise results (vocational courses, intensive test tutoring, strategic exclusions) and thus reverse or stave off a negative inspection judgement. As a result of such actions he could, he suggested, create time and space to get on with the real and slow business of school change.

The power game involved in simulation/compliance/resistance features in a recent report written about 'light touch inspection' for the Association of School and College Leaders (ASCL).[28] It suggests that schools can be 'ambushed' by inspectors if they are not aware of, and cannot answer questions about, all of the data that is now available in the newly developed on-line databases used by inspection teams. Postcolonial scholar Tomasz Szkudlarek addresses such power games, and notes that acts of resistance may invite acts of repression, whereas simulation may well create space for the creation of strategies of

[24]See Jill Blackmore and Judyth Sachs, *Performing and Reforming Leaders* and Pat Thomson, 'How Principals Lose "Face": A Disciplinary Tale of Educational Administration and Modern Managerialism', *Discourse* 22, no. 1 (2001): 5–22; Pat Thomson, 'Severed Heads and Compliant Bodies? A Speculation about Principal Identities', *Discourse* 25, no. 1 (2004): 301–20; Pat Thomson, *School Leadership – Heads on the Block?* (London: Routledge, in press).

[25]John Smyth and Alastair Dow, 'What's Wrong with Outcomes? Spotter Planes, Action Plans and Steerage of the Educational Workplace', *British Journal of Sociology of Education* 19, no. 3 (1998): 291–304.

[26]Interviews conducted for a national project examining the take-up of creativity by schools, a long-term ethnography, and a corpus of interviews conducted with heads over 10 years.

[27]See Marie Stubbs, *Ahead of the Class. How an Inspiring Headmistress Gave Children Back Their Future* (London: John Murray, 2003).

[28]*Times Educational Supplement*, September 21, 2007, p. 26. The report featured quotes from the paper's writer, Dr Peter Kent, headteacher of Lawrence Sheriff School, Rugby.

resistance or opposition.[29] In the three specific instances just outlined this was precisely what the heads understood to be the case. The negative consequences that they feared were both for their schools and themselves. In the English context, failure to 'perform' as required can result in: individual sacking or forced retirement of the headteacher; media demonisation; collapse of parent trust in the school; and ultimately, school closure.[30]

But simulation is not an easy game to play. Policy is continually adjusted to take account of its own weaknesses. For example, in England, recent shifts in inspection and audit regimes such as the development of school 'self-evaluations' and the shift to create GCSE targets based on core and not vocational subjects, have closed down the options for simulation that some secondary heads, like 'the fixer', had adopted. If this is not to be understood as a simple conspiracy, then an analysis which moves beyond the descriptive is required. Studies of policy as discourse and of headteacher agency as discursive might explicate the power games in operation in such policy shifts. They might also probe whether surveillance regimes not only construct heads as self-managing forensic subjects but also whether simulations and critiques of audit requirements ironically normalise their acceptance.

Acting counter to policy?

However, despite the possible consequences some heads *do* appear to resist, that is, act overtly against policy.

Holly Tree Primary is situated in a Midlands city.[31] It has 300-plus children on roll and 60-plus in the nursery. Half the children live in local authority housing on the two council estates close to the school. A higher than average percentage of children qualifies for free school meals (24%). The school has a reputation as successful, and inspection reports which deem it 'outstanding'.[32] Miriam, the head teacher, ran the school since it started over 30 years ago and was, until her retirement in late 2005, one of the longest serving headteachers in England.

When the Literacy Hour was introduced into English primary schools, Holly Tree was one of those that did not conform because Miriam and the most senior staff believed that it would actually reduce time on literacy, as well as work counter to the full range of literate practices. They maintained a focus on literature, process and genre writing, and introduced some elements of direct instruction. They refused to change their timetable to feature a specific daily slot called literacy.

---

[29]Tomasz Szkudlarek, *The Problem of Freedom in Postmodern Education* (Westport, CT: Bergin & Garvey, 1993).

[30]For a graphic Australian example see Martin Forsey, *Challenging the System? A Dramatic Tale of Neoliberal Reform in an Australian High School* (Charlotte, NC: Information Age Publishing, 2007).

[31]Chris Hall, Lisa Russell and I conducted a three-year ethnographic study of the school, two years of which were funded by the ESRC. See for example: Christine Hall and Pat Thomson, 'Creative Partnerships? Cultural Policy and Inclusive Arts Practices in One Primary School', *British Educational Research Journal* 33, no. 3 (2007): 315–29; Christine Hall, Pat Thomson, and Lisa Russell, 'Teaching Like an Artist: the Pedagogic Identities and Practices of Artists in Schools', *British Journal of Sociology of Education* 28, no. 5 (2007): 605–19; Pat Thomson, Christine Hall, and Lisa Russell, 'An Arts Project Failed, Censored or…? A Critical Incident Approach to Artist–School Partnerships', *Changing English* 13, no. 1 (2006): 29–44; Pat Thomson, Christine Hall, and Lisa Russell, 'If These Walls Could Speak: Reading Displays of Primary Children's Work', *Ethnography and Education* 3, no. 3 (2007): 381–400.

[32]The actual reports cannot be named because this would reveal the identity of the school.

Miriam was able to discuss refusal to comply with the most powerful figure in OfSTED at the time and used the school's performance as the justification for her refusal to adhere to the Literacy Hour.

> Miriam: They can't pick me off as long as my results are good. And I knew that from the very beginning. I mean Chris Woodhead came into school and he said: 'Oh, you don't have to do it if your results are good'. And our results are good.

Miriam says that the school focused strongly on process: how things were taught rather than what was taught. It did not contest literacy per se, but developed/maintained a counter-policy pedagogical practice. It provided what was mandated and aimed to do it well, but did so in its own way. But it also attempted to add to what was required.

> Deputy Elena: ...it is all about exploring outside of the entitlement, if you like. We know what those children have to receive; we know what their entitlement is. Every QCA [Qualifications and Curriculum Authority] document tells us what the entitlement is for each Year group. But it's then building around it, isn't it, an enriched programme of learning.

There was in Holly Tree a strong narrative about principled resistance to policies that were deemed antithetical to 'good teaching'.

> Elena: ...being able to say: 'We know what is best for our children. We feel strongly about this. We can deliver what you're asking us to deliver and more if you leave us to organise it in our own way'. And proving it. That's right. Proving that there hasn't been a fall in standards. And the rigour has still to be there but the flexibility has to be there as well. With trialling and to be able to prove what you say and to stand your ground and say: 'We know this works because'. And we've had to have a firm case for doing it but then having had a firm case to be able to stand up for ourselves and say that we know what we are talking about.

The senior staff believed that if the school's results were to slip then an apparently acquiescent inspection system might not remain sympathetic. Performance on tests and inspections was important to Holly Tree, because failure to do well would threaten school autonomy and bring unwanted interference in the ways in which they operated. They therefore kept a very careful eye on test results and took remedial action if they showed any sign of slippage. Thus, paradoxically, in order to 'buck the system', the school had to demonstrate that it did not.

This Holly Tree exemplar suggests that schools like Holly Tree and heads like Miriam both resist and comply at the same time – it is not a question of one or the other, but rather how/when they do both at once. Acts of resistance by any individual headteacher or school are strongly framed and contained, and thus action against policy is always constrained and delimited. If the dominant policy 'pick and choose' approach that headteachers report can be called mediation, it is mediation within profound limits. It is a distinctly corralled form of agency but is agency nevertheless. And it is in the Holly Tree case an agency that produces an education that is much more enjoyable and engaging for pupils.

Theorising the logic of headteachers' practice might also take a case like this further to see whether the assumption of autonomy is a taken-for-granted truth, a misrecognition of schooling's (re)productive practices and a necessary disposition which maintains hierarchised power relations.

Speaking out against policy

Heads however do not restrict themselves to local actions with/against policy. Individual heads critical of aspects of government policy are often quoted in major educational media publications. One issue of the *Times Educational Supplement* (21 September 2007) illustrates the point. This single issue contains three 'critique' items:

(1) A report of a survey of headteachers' workload[33] shows a small improvement in the workload of secondary heads and a marginal worsening of the situation for primary. In the article Mike Griffiths, head of the Northampton School for Boys, described also as a member of the ASCL, is quoted as saying about the excess of paperwork 'At 11 o'clock at night, with a glass of wine, it's quite easy to chuck a lot of it in the bin' (p. 19).

(2) A column written by Mike Kent, headteacher of Comber Grove Primary in Camberwell (p. 33), takes issue with paper-driven systems of performance management. He was, he wrote, recommended by OfSTED to conduct formal assessments of staff without which he could not demonstrate he had a system for monitoring teaching and learning. 'So for half a term I did just that. I became an inspector rather than a resource, and I learned nothing about my teachers and classrooms that I didn't know already. Then I went back to doing what I knew worked best.'
Kent asserts that the problem with performance management is that it is a system which lacks trust in teachers. A breakout box in the column says 'What I refuse to do is sit in the corner of a classroom ticking boxes on the teacher's performance'.

(3) A further column (p. 31) written by Geoff Barton, Head of King Edward VI school in Suffolk, is sardonic about the policy of federations of schools '…a successful school takes over a less successful one in a kind of franchise arrangement and the head is suddenly recast in the role of executive chef, travelling between kitchens to taste the consommé and bark expletives'.
But Barton is more concerned about the 'scandal' of many 16-year-olds' failure in GSCEs and the knock-on effects for unemployment and life opportunities. Sheeting home the blame to a 'curriculum straitjacket' he proposes 'a small number of national targets' combined with the 'trust, flexibility, and freedom to innovate'.

Here then in a single issue of the *Times Educational Supplement* are three head teachers not only engaged in public criticism of audit systems but two also openly confess their refusal to comply, presumably inviting sanctions. It is important to note that none of these three heads comes from a school which is 'vulnerable' to allegations of poor student performance, and, like Miriam at Holly Tree, they are also experienced headteachers. It seems fair to assume that they are confident in their own ways of doing things, and able to argue their point of view with officers representing official policy mandates. It is also not unreasonable to assume that the three would have calculated that speaking out was unlikely to cause them or their schools immediate harm.

A clue to this calculation lies in the timing of the three 'speaking out' articles. The same *Times Educational Supplement* reports in its lead article a 'mass protest' to the House of Commons Education and Skills Select Committee about testing. If the *Times Educational Supplement* is to be believed, there is mounting pressure on the government to change

[33]Reporting on Helen Angle, Nicholas Gilbey, and Mark Belcher, *Teachers' Workload Diary Survey. March 2007* (London: Office of Manpower Economics, School Teachers Review Board, 2007).

policy. The general secretary of the ASCL noted via the *Times Educational Supplement* 'Everyone except the Government recognises that the current system is unsustainable. With the new Prime Minister we have the best chance that we have ever had' (p. 1).

The very same week, the National Democrats also launched their education policy platform which included promises about reductions in the testing regime. The National Association of Headteachers (NAHT) had also just declared a 'war on bureaucracy'. Not only was the NAHT campaign likely to garner considerable public sympathy as well as a great deal of collective activity in schools but also heads caught speaking out might well have had considerable support from all over the political spectrum. This is because complaints against excessive regulation, paperwork and red-tape has resonance across the political spectrum,[34] and strong historical antecedents in critiques of the welfare state.[35]

The temporal co-location of heads 'speaking truth to power' with movement in the political sphere, increasing public criticism, and a great deal of 'special interest group' organisation, points to the wider cultural context in which critique and resistance occur. Heads I have interviewed confirm that there are times and occasions when it seems possible for those who are literally well placed (that is those who work in schools relatively protected against snap audit judgements based on test results) to speak out against policy. One of those occasions is when their voices are in tune with a groundswell of concern, and another is when they speak as union members for their association's policy.

It is thus not always the case that speaking out produces reprisals. It is when individual heads appear to speak for many others that they are 'safe'. Studies which looked at policy as discursive might identify the shifting power relations which legitimate headteachers' voices, about what, at what times and for what purposes.

Beyond the individual

Jean Anyon has persuasively argued that major changes in postwar US educational policy have been the result of the actions of social movements[36] – broad-based organisational coalitions such as the civil rights movement and the radical Christian revivalist movement. Her analysis is based in social science theorisations which show that individuals acting alone do not bring about major change.[37] Even small-scale reforms are produced through a complex interplay of scales, actors, histories and ideologies, in which the vast majority of policy actors are collectives. From this perspective, it seems relatively unproductive for leadership/management scholars to simply look to the actions of individual headteachers for evidence of resistance to and critique of policy agendas, and imperative to look to their collective activities.

[34]Neoconservatism, for example, is strongly any anti-state regulation, while a social democratic politics argues for democratic accountability. Both positions might support a 'war on bureaucracy'.

[35]Christopher Hood, *The Art of the State. Culture, Rhetoric and Public Management* (Oxford: Clarendon Press, 1998).

[36]Jean Anyon, *Radical Possibilities. Public Policy, Urban Education and a New Social Movement* (New York: Routledge, 2005).

[37]For example, Ulrich Beck, *The Reinvention of Politics. Rethinking Modernity in the Global Social Order* (Cambridge: Polity Press, 1997); Nancy Fraser, *Justice Interruptus. Critical Reflections on the 'Postsocialist' Condition* (London: Routledge, 1997); Michael Maffesoli, *The Time of the Tribes: The Decline of Individualism in Mass Societies* (Thousand Oaks, CA: Sage, 1995); Alberto Mellucci, *Challenging Codes. Collective Action in the Information Age* (Cambridge: Cambridge University Press, 1996).

One new collective option for headteachers is the network. The English Labour government has deliberately sponsored the development of networks, loose configurations of schools which share experiences and which 'coach and mentor' each other.[38] This is the organisational form of the future, it is contended,[39] whose prime goal is mutual learning, framed and shaped by existing and anticipated policy.[40] This networking activity is approvingly discussed and promoted in policy documents. In England, networking is arguably an organisational form which does not so much challenge policy but manage 'bespoke' implementation and it does require ongoing critical attention from education and management scholars.[41]

However, the field also needs to widen its gaze to consider the ongoing collective activities of headteachers' associations, who work at local, regional and national level not simply to implement policy, but also to influence it.

A collective voice: headteacher associations

I was once an elected President of a principals' association – the South Australian Secondary Principals Association to be precise. At the time, this was simply an association since all heads in the state also belonged to the Australian Education Union. This was true in all Australian states except Victoria where the majority of heads left the Australian Education Union to form their own union, a move concurrent with devolution of authority to schools and the formation of a new separate award structure.[42]

In South Australia the principals' associations was reform-oriented and negotiated formal representation on all policymaking committees and bodies, and thus association meetings largely consisted of organising consultations with members, writing position papers and formulating strategies through both subcommittees and an elected Executive.[43] Large numbers of principals were involved in the web of committees, and it was thus the case that the vast majority in the state exercised 'system leadership' – *and* used that term to describe their/our activities.[44] Media commentary was handled by the President who also enjoyed ready access to senior Departmental officers. In my time in office the association was particularly active around modified proposals for devolution, resource issues, the nature

[38]Wiel Veugelers and Mary John O'Hair, eds., *Network Learning for Organisational Change* (Buckingham, UK: Open University Press, 2006).
[39]G.F. Thompson, *Between Hierarchies and Markets: The Logic and Limits of Network Forms of Organisation* (Oxford: Oxford University Press, 2003).
[40]See 'next practice' at http://www.innovation-unit.co.uk (accessed November 20, 2007).
[41]David Hartley, 'The New Managerialism in Education: A Mission Impossible?', *Cambridge Journal of Education* 27, no. 1 (1997): 47–57.
[42]See critical accounts in Pam Bishop and Bill Mulford, 'When Will They Ever Learn? Another Failure of Centrally-imposed Change', *School Leadership and Management* 19, no. 2 (1999): 179–87; Jill Blackmore, Chris Bigum, John Hodgens, and Louise Laskey, 'Managed Change and Self-management in *Schools of the Future*', *Leading and Managing* 2, no. 3 (1996): 195–220; and advocacy in Brian Caldwell and Don Hayward, *The Future of Schools* (London: Falmer, 1997).
[43]There was an association for each sector and a joint associations Executive.
[44]The term seems to have been recently discovered in the UK where it is used to denote activities undertaken on behalf of the government (see http://www.ncsl.org.uk/publications/publications-systemleadership.cfm, last accessed November 12, 2007), rather than the more political/critical role that I am describing.

of principals' work[45] and the successful development of a local leadership centre and national professional association professional development programme.[46] The association was a significant policy player, since departmental executive officers and the government minister recognised that, in the absence of a strong system of audit and sanctions, policy had little chance of implementation without principals' active support.

While different, headteachers' associations in the UK are also highly significant in policy making. My argument here is that their role is worthy of investigation and that what they do is to neither simply comply nor resist. To make this point I provide some indicative information based on conference resolutions made public via the website of one headteacher's association and an interview with an official spokesperson. It is important to note here that when unions exercise opposition to policy they do so via representative means – through motions and official, elected spokespersons. While unions do consist of thousands of members, with myriad personal opinions, they politically speak with one voice in the public arena. Thus, investigations of professional associations need to both consider the ways in which political decisions are made, but also the ways in which decisions, once made, are effected politically. Here I consider the latter, and is important to recognise that the official here is not speaking for himself, but is speaking as the union, and is officially employed to do so. I reiterate that this next section does not claim to be rigorous research into headteachers' associations but rather is intended to indicate why it might be important.

Here I briefly consider the officially and democratically determined political role of one UK headteachers' association, the NAHT, drawing on an interview with Mick Brookes, the elected, full-time NAHT general secretary, a former and very experienced primary school headteacher.[47] His name is used with permission.

The NAHT as policy actor

The NAHT is one of two headteachers' associations in the UK. It has 28,500 members, headteachers, deputy and assistant headteachers, the majority of whom work in the primary school sector. The NAHT does however cover all sectors of schooling. Describing itself as 'the largest organisation of its kind in Europe' (NAHT website), it is a union which offers a full suite of services – professional development and professional magazine, individual membership benefits, assistance with inspection and performance management, international linkages, individual legal support, political lobbying and salary negotiation. It also commissions surveys and some research, sometimes in concert with the other major headteacher union, the ASCL.[48]

The NAHT has recently re-entered the 'social partnership', which Brookes describes as the

[45]See, for example, Pat Thomson, *Local Decision Making and Management* (Adelaide, South Australia: Joint Principals Associations, 1994); Pat Thomson, *The Changing Role of the School Principal* (Adelaide, South Australia: South Australian Secondary Principals Association, 1997); Pat Thomson and Phil Wilkins, *Survey of Spending in DSP Schools* (Adelaide, South Australia: Joint Principals Associations, 1997).

[46]See Centre for Leaders at http://www.cle.decs.sagov.au and for national professional development http://www.apapdc.edu.au.

[47]The interview has been transcribed and coded as is customary practice.

[48]For example, Centre for Teacher and School Development, University of Nottingham, and National Association of Head Teachers, 'Class Size Research and the Quality of Education', 1998, http://acorn.educ.nottingham.ac.uk/SchEd/res/exec.htm (accessed March 2, 1999).

> …mechanism set up by government four or five years ago, intended to revolutionise the way in which the unions in the education sphere came to education policy. So rather than the old collective bargaining situation, policy was developed along with teacher associations…

The partnership entails an intensive commitment to dialogue on the part of unions and government.

> We meet once a week, so it's pretty heavy duty and with an awful lot of papers that come that need to be ratified in between time.

The vast majority of education government initiatives are made available to the partnership to discuss and many are formally endorsed by the partnership members. However, the government clearly runs the partnership.

> …the minister has sway over what is and isn't said … but that said some good things come out of it as well as some disasters…

The NAHT pulled out of the social partnership for nearly a year over its opposition to lack of resourcing for the introduction of primary planning time for teachers, but Brookes sees this period as being 'tricky', and a possible reason why 'the teachers have done better than heads' out of the arrangement.[49] The NAHT recently re-entered the partnership 'on the proviso that there would be research into whether schools had sufficient resources to institute planning time'.

Despite not always agreeing with policy or getting what they want out of the process, Brookes suggests that the NAHT sees the partnership as a forum to not only approve and actively influence but also to counter specific policy directions. An example of this can be seen in their position on the new forms of school organisation and headship – federations, co-principalships and the like – suggested as one means of making the job of headship more do-able.[50]

> A lot of the social partnership is about school leadership which brings us nicely to where we want to be – but it's about different models of school leadership and our line is to say, yes that's all very well but when you were looking at problems of recruitment for teachers, the immediate effect was to see how we could reduce the workload for teachers. The reaction to the headteachers has been 'if you can't stand the heat get out of the kitchen'. Well an awful lot of them are – and very few want to come in … we are saying you have to look at retention before you can look at recruitment…

This view, that attention to headteacher working conditions ought to be the prime focus for policy, is taken into important fora other than the social partnership, for example, into dealings with the National College for School Leadership (NCSL) who both influence and carry out policy.

> We actually had an interesting conversation (with the NCSL) about effective models of school leadership and we made the point that that's actually a very sloppy use of language, it's not about effective models of schools it's about *appropriate* models of schools which will enable school leaders to work effectively.

[49]The National Union of Teachers (NUT) has consistently refused to join the partnership as one manifestation of its opposition to New Labour's agenda.
[50]See Michael Bristow, Gillian Ireson, and Andy Coleman, *A Life in the Day of a Headteacher. A Study of Practice and Wellbeing* (Nottingham: NCSL, 2007).

Concerns about work practices and conditions are also translated into independent association activities, one of which is the recent campaign against red-tape and unnecessary bureaucracy mentioned earlier in this article. The NAHT sees the campaign not only as political lobbying, and a way of drawing attention to the paper overload required of headteachers, but also, according to Brookes, as

> …strengthening the resolve of members to say 'no thanks, thanks very much for that but we don't want that, that's a lot more work and I can't see how that's going to benefit our children and so we are not going to do it'.

The NAHT, he suggests, wants to see an end to

> …inappropriate tasks which take heads away from the strategic leadership of learning and planning … it is a nonsense to say that they effectively prefer to clean out the loos rather than focus on teaching … that doesn't sound to me like a career choice…

Brookes argues that the current tranche of audit and performance requirements – which create headteachers' overwork, act as a disincentive to recruitment and retention, and create adverse teaching and learning conditions in schools – arise from the lack of trust in teachers. The union therefore chose the slogan 'It's time to trust schools' for their 2007 annual conference. Brookes sees the NAHT role in the social partnership as helping to build up that trust, but also believes it can do more.

Brookes suggested that a headteachers' organisation needs to be concerned with more than salaries and political lobbying, and so on behalf of the organisation he was in discussion with a private-sector company about running services for those schools which do not have the means to afford their own business management infrastructure.

> …because if we can do that and can provide or we can commission the services, commission is a better word, then you are going to reduce the stress of working at schools and that's good for the kids and that's good for education. That's where I see a modern trade union coming in … it's saying our members have an integrity of purpose which is about education and we are here to facilitate our members' needs which is also facilitating education because it makes life easier for school leaders to lead, they lead better and our schools are better … create the conditions for good practice.

In doing this, he suggested, the NAHT was moving away from simply providing individual services to members, to brokering new services for schools. This is a fascinating issue which is deserving of serious investigation, suggesting as it does, a new interpretation of the kinds of services that unions routinely provide for their members and one which intersects with contemporary privatisation agendas.[51]

Unions generally provide a collective perspective on the concerns that members, in this case headteachers, are individually only sometimes able to advance in public (as argued earlier). NAHT policy resolutions for the last few years have consistently called for an end to unnecessary testing and league tables (see Figure 1) and their views are entirely consistent with much of the critique made by many educational researchers, albeit expressed more colourfully.

[51]Steven Ball, *Education PLC. Understanding Private Sector Participation in Public Sector Education* (London: Routledge, 2007).

2007 We demand that Council ensure that English schools have the same equality of rights as schools in Wales, in that we should be held in the same professional regard as our colleagues and, like them, be able to assess the children through teacher assessment.
2006 Conference deplores the continuing growth of an educational system that is systems led, test driven, data obsessed, centrally controlled and governed by bean counters, Conference calls upon Council actively to campaign against this pointless, demotivating and destructive regime.
2005 All schools are disadvantaged by the value added process, the system needs changing.
2004 NAHT believes that the children now in our schools are the most tested generation of this countryís history and calls upon the Westminster government to reduce drastically this culture of testing everything that moves.

Figure 1. Samples of NAHT policy (from the NAHT website).

Given these views, the range of activity that they undertake, and the *educational* concerns on which headteacher associations speak and act, it could be expected that they might feature in the educational leadership and management literatures. The NAHT's Mick Brookes certainly asserts that headteachers' associations *are* players in the formation of policy, providing specific input not simply about the self-interests of school leaders, but also on the widest range of education policy issues. However, very few educational leadership and management scholars have taken the role and the critical voice of headteachers' associations as worthy of study. The ways in which they work to represent heads are largely unexamined.

Taking the critical voice of headteachers seriously

One exception to this lacuna is Thrupp who devotes a chapter in his critique of Official School Improvement to contestation.[52] Half of this chapter (Chapter 5) is dedicated to a discussion of the collective critical actions of unions and professional associations. These are described as 'varying considerably' in their approach to 'issues that go wider than pay and working conditions'. Thrupp suggests that membership support for action against testing or inspections '…may be limited because the established reforms have become acceptable to members and because openly refusing to comply could have serious consequences'.[53]

[52]Martin Thrupp, *School Improvement: An Unofficial Approach* (London: Continuum, 2005).
[53]Ibid., 81.

In the case of the NAHT at least, given their continued policy resolutions against testing, inspection and so on, the latter appears more likely to be the case. But it will take systematic research to get beyond speculation about what might be happening.

The brief indicative snapshot of the NAHT given in this article suggests that it does more than verbalise opposition and/or rubber stamp government decisions. Its official spokesperson claims to be taking an increasingly active role in developing alternatives to policy. Of course, speaking out and arguing for major reform does not constitute overt resistance of the kind undertaken by social movements, and as advocated by Anyon.[54] But while what they do might not be called resistance, the political actions of the NAHT are not clearly not simply complying with policy. Understanding precisely what headteachers unions do will require sustained scholarly engagement.

I have argued elsewhere that headteachers' associations are not ill-disposed to academics.[55] They do not see the professional development that their associations provide, nor that provided through the NCSL, as being all that needs to be available. Nor are they hostile to research, although they can afford to commission very little of it for themselves. In interview Mick Brookes, for example, continually referred to findings from research, and also spoke affirmatively of his own postgraduate experiences and understandings. This may of course have been because he was speaking to an academic, but the interview transcript suggests something more habituated about his references to 'evidence' and 'ideas' than a one-shot performance. How far he is indicative of his staff colleagues and of the wider membership is of course unknown, but given this from the official spokesperson, the scholarly community has some reason to assume the likelihood of a sustained conversation.

However, the continued myopia within the field to the existence and activities of headteachers' associations works against potentially productive relationships. We could make headteachers' associations an important site of study in their own right.[56] An analysis of headteacher associations in the context of the educational and wider social field – and/or examining them as social movements through a focus on the motivation to take part, collective identity building and forms of action – would allow a more nuanced and critical discussion of the potentials of their collective organisations to effect widespread educational change.

In addition to researching the role and operation of headteachers' associations, the leadership/management field might also seek them out as research collaborators and partners, but not simply see them as alternative sources of funds. We could for example consult with headteachers' associations over areas for research which would provide strategic evidence for policymaking or for understanding the everyday work of school leadership and management. We might invite local headteachers' association branches to form reference groups for

---

[54]Anyon, *Radical Possibilities*. Social movements typically act as 'counterpublics' (see Fraser, *Justice Interruptus*) either because 'they have been excluded from the public sphere or because they reject the norms that operate within it' (p. 43; Marion Barnes, Janet Newman, and Helen Sullivan, *Power, Participation and Political Renewal. Case Studies in Public Participation*, Bristol: The Policy Press, 2007). The return of the NAHT to the social partnership might be read as a 'returning to the tent' to engage in reform, rather than make alliances with other organisations interested in overt resistance. But it is important to note the post-Thatcher legacy has largely curtailed overt resistance in any form by any organisation. It is not reasonable in my view to criticise one organisation for a more general phenomenon.

[55]Pat Thomson, 'Move Over Rover. An Essay/Assay of the Field of Educational Management and Leadership in the UK', *Journal of Education Policy* 15, no. 6 (2000): 717–32.

[56]Teacher unions for example are studied in this way.

research projects.[57] We might also include headteachers' associations as important expert informants to our research, use headteachers' association publications as sources of information and expert opinion, and run invitational seminars for headteachers' association members about research which has important policy implications.

In sum

I have suggested that in the leadership/management field, headteacher agency is under-theorised and de-historicised. I have proposed that the broader field of social science has helpful resources to offer which might allow different understandings of the individual acts of headteacher resistance and critique that do occur. I have also argued that if leadership/management scholars do not seriously engage with the collective organisation of head-teachers' associations then we not only fail to map and understand more fully the ways in which policy is made and enacted, but we also alienate ourselves from the very group that we seek to work with to build well-theorised leadership/management practice.

Acknowledgements

Thanks to Christine Hall and Lisa Russell for permission to use the Holly Tree exemplar.

[57] When my colleagues and I did just this on an ARC project examining principal supply in Australia, we were directed to the principal selection process, something we had not originally included in our research design: see Jill Blackmore, Pat Thomson, and Karin Barty, 'Principal Selection: Homosociability, the Search for Security and the Production of Normalised Principal Identities', *Educational Management, Administration and Leadership* 34, no. 3 (2006): 297–337.

Good intentions are not enough: a critical examination of diversity and educational leadership scholarship

Jane Wilkinson

Introduction

A central conundrum within the emerging field of theory and practice in diversity and educational leadership is why many studies avert their gaze from a critical examination of leadership's role in either constructing and perpetuating structural inequalities, or alternatively, challenging and interrogating them. As DiTomaso and Hooijberg observe, one would expect that the 'study of diversity would be all about leadership, but this is not what has developed'.[1] Moreover, when diversity is examined in relation to Anglocentric norms of leadership, most often it is constructed as the property of an (non-white, non-Anglo) 'other', which is to be managed by (white, frequently masculine and middle class) educational leaders.[2] Less often is the spotlight shone on leadership's own homogeneity, be it in relation to ethnicity or other structural factors such as class or gender. Why might this be the case?

In this article these puzzles are examined through a mapping of key diversity discourses in organisational management and critical feminist scholarship. I then analyse how such discourses are being applied in nascent work about diversity and educational leadership. Drawing upon ongoing black, Indigenous and critical feminist scholarship

---

[1]Nancy DiTomaso and Robert Hooijberg, 'Diversity and the Demands of Leadership', *Leadership Quarterly* 7, no. 2 (1996): 163.
[2]Jane Wilkinson, 'Examining Representations of Women's Leadership in the Media and Australian Universities' (PhD diss., Deakin University, 2005).

around the politics of difference,[3] I argue that one of the potential dangers of emerging research for diversity and educational leadership is a slippage into an apolitical and instrumentalist focus upon diversity as a form of management containment of individuals. Instead, the article takes seriously recent calls for the need to work with notions of diversity and leadership in ways that are conceptually rich, socially just, educationally transformative,[4] as well as critically reflexive.[5]

As part of this reflexive turn, I briefly note two points. Firstly, engaging in critique and scholarship in the field of diversity and difference is difficult and at times, hostile territory to traverse.[6] As a scholar of mixed Anglo-Celtic and Eastern European origins living in the post-colonial nation of Australia, I am acutely aware of the privilege that my whiteness confers upon me. Hence, in analysing diversity discourses in the educational leadership field, I do not wish to set myself up as a white 'expert'; nor to be seen to be as advocating an 'add ethnic minority to the shopping list of educational leadership and stir' approach. Secondly, the term 'diversity' in countries such as the UK signifies a synonym for minority (non-white, non-Anglo) ethnicity.[7] Though at times adopting this definition in the article, I also attempt to problematise and denaturalise it through a deconstruction of how such discourses are articulated in the educational leadership field. In so doing, I aim to render explicit the ethnocentric assumptions, which underpin these taken-for-granted definitions.

The article commences by examining two recent and contrasting diversity trends, drawn from very different disciplinary and historical traditions, that is, American management literature based upon the private sector; and black and critical feminist scholarship on diversity and difference. Both have influenced how diversity has been taken up in studies of educational leadership. However, due to profoundly different orientations, they have had quite contrasting material effects in terms of practices and constructions of educational leadership, particularly vis-á-vis research in the field. Then drawing upon recent scholarship which maps how diversity discourses are made manifest in educational leadership as a field of enquiry and practice,[8] I examine how they are applied in two recent articles published in *International Studies in Education*. In so doing, I adopt the definition of discourse as 'a practice not just of representing the world, but of signifying the world, constituting and constructing the world in meaning'.[9] On this basis, diversity discourses are not givens but political constructs that are constantly being remade through leaders and scholars' own practices and ways of speaking, researching and leading in key sites of social knowledge production and practice, such as schools and universities. Hence, the knowledge that is produced by scholars and practitioners in the field in regard to diversity may serve to

---

[3]For example, bell hooks, *Talking Back: Thinking Feminist, Thinking Black* (Boston: South End Press, 1989); Heidi Safia Mirza, 'Black Women in Higher Education: Defining a Space/Finding a Place', in *Feminist Academics: Creative Agents for Change*, ed. Louise Morley and Val Walsh (London: Taylor & Francis, 1995), 145–55; Georgina Tsolidis, *Schooling, Diaspora and Gender: Being Feminist and Being Different* (Buckingham, UK: University Press, 2001).

[4]Jill Blackmore, 'Deconstructing Diversity Discourses in the Field of Educational Management and Leadership', *Educational Management Administration & Leadership* 34, no. 2 (2006): 181–99.

[5]Marlene Morrison, Jacky Lumby, and Krishan Sood, 'Diversity and Diversity Management: Messages from Recent Research', *Educational Management Administration & Leadership* 34, no. 3 (2006): 277–95.

[6]Tanya Fitzgerald, 'Changing the Deafening Silence of Indigenous Women's Voices in Educational Leadership', *Journal of Educational Administration* 41, no. 1 (2003): 13.

[7]Jacky Lumby with Marianne Coleman, *Leadership and Diversity: Challenging Theory and Practice in Education* (London: Sage, 2007), 1.

[8]Blackmore, 'Deconstructing Diversity Discourses'.

[9]Norman Fairclough, *Discourse and Social Change* (Cambridge: Polity Press, 1992), 64.

entrench asymmetrical power structures through monocultural, majority ethnic leadership constructs and practices. Alternatively, it may extend and expand notions of leadership in ways that are socially just and genuinely inclusive. In brief, good intentions are not enough in the complex and challenging field of leadership and diversity as the following analysis reveals.

Does the innocent face of diversity belie the serpent underneath?

There exists a range of different readings of diversity, including 'productive diversity' which emphasises 'negotiated difference'[10] and 'civic pluralism';[11] and the framing of diversity within a concept of social justice, which aims to challenge and transform the culture of organisations rather than assimilating people within them.[12] Which discourses are privileged at particular moments within education or other fields will depend upon the political, economic and historical contexts of the time. Hence, a third discourse drawn from the American business management field became a pervasive thread in educational policies and texts in Anglo nations such as Australia in the 1990s, where a largely neoliberal agenda had come to dominate educational policy-making. The 'corporate discourse' of diversity[13] emerged in Australia through a series of key reports into management commissioned by the Federal Government in the mid-1990s.[14] As opposed to the emphasis upon social transformation, arising from earlier civil rights movements, the corporate discourse focuses upon an individualising notion of difference. Making the most of one's (ethnically, or in Australian terms, also gender diverse) workplaces is posited as making good business sense. Diversity is viewed as a commodity, which, if harnessed productively, can lead to greater profits. Hence, so the argument goes, managing diversity utilises the talents and skills of the variety of individuals within one's workplace.[15] The danger with the application of the latter approach in both scholarship and practice is that it depoliticises leadership as a construct and denudes it of transformative potential. It frames diversity purely as a management tool, shorn of any genuine commitment to significant organisational transformation in the structural inequities such as gender, 'race' and class, which bedevil schooling and universities as key sites of social reproduction.[16] Yet, given the current emphasis in Anglophone education systems upon corporate principles, cost-efficiency, competition and individual 'choice', it connotes an appropriate fit with the prevailing logic of the English-speaking education field.[17]

---

[10]Bill Cope and Mary Kalantzis, *Productive Diversity: A New, Australian Model for Work and Management* (Sydney: Pluto Press Australia, 1997).
[11]Carol Bacchi, 'Managing Equity: Mainstreaming and "Diversity" in Australian Universities', in *Gender and the Restructured University*, ed. Ann Brooks and Alison Mackinnon (Buckingham, UK: The Society for Research into Higher Education and Open University Press, 2001), 119–35.
[12]Ibid.
[13]Blackmore, 'Deconstructing Diversity Discourses', 181, 184.
[14]David Karpin, *Enterprising Nation: Renewing Australia's Managers to Meet the Challenges of the Asia-Pacific Century: Report of the Industry Task Force on Leadership and Management Skills* (Canberra: Australian Commonwealth Government, Department of Employment, Education and Training, 1995); Clare Burton and Carolyn Ryall, *Enterprising Nation: Renewing Australia's Managers to Meet the Challenges of the Asia-Pacific Century: Managing Diversity* (Canberra: Australian Commonwealth Government, Department of Employment, Education and Training, 1995).
[15]Bacchi, 'Managing Equity'.
[16]Ibid.
[17]Ibid.

Clearly, diversity is not an unproblematic concept and elicits a spectrum of interpretations, with varying views of its material effects. Black feminist educational scholars such as Heidi Safia Mirza argue that in countries such as England, there has been an *apparent* diminution in the importance of 'race' as a factor in education. She asserts that in a manner similar to the corporate discourse of diversity, the uncritical, apolitical and individualising take up of 'merit' as a discourse in educational policies and practices, leads to a 'colour-blind approach … [where] … we are told we are all the same' with '[f]air treatment … based on merit'. However, as she notes, not 'all have the same equal opportunities to get that merit'.[18] One of the material effects of merit/colour-blind discourses is that they fail to highlight the complex ways in which other structural factors such as class, gender and location intersect in educational debates around, for example, students' academic achievements in basic skills tests. Rather, Mirza contends that the employment of new and seemingly innocuous phrases such as 'ethnicity' and 'cultural differences' to explain differences in achievement in such tests between different groups of students may potentially carry out the same kinds of symbolic labour/violence that terms such as 'race' have signified in the past. Thus, she asserts, a form of racism is produced which by its very subtleness is more difficult to challenge.[19] Heidi Safia Mirza's interrogation of how merit discourses may translate into implicit forms of racism in education, when applied apolitically and with an individualising focus, has illuminating parallels with the application of corporate discourses of diversity in relation to educational leadership. Moreover, it has specific implications in terms of more critical scholarly approaches to notions of 'difference' as outlined in the next section.

Mirza's assertion that in contemporary England, a new form of 'cultural racism' had emerged surreptitiously from colour- (and gender) blind notions of merit, poses a major counterargument to the key diversity management text of the early 1990s[20] from which the corporate discourse of diversity had originated.[21] Telling entitled, *Beyond Race and Gender: Unleashing the Power of Your Total Workforce by Unleashing Diversity*, the text signals a deliberate shift from (the potentially threatening in management terms) identification of groups based upon inequity such as 'race' or gender.[22] Instead, utilising more innocuous terms, it exhorts management to examine, '"the many ways employees are different and the many ways they are alike"'.[23] The notion of equivalence between all (individuals) and the denial of special status for specific disadvantaged groups was a siren song which many private- and public-sector organisations were happy to heed in the increasingly neoliberal regimes of the American corporate sector and the managerialist public sector of Anglophone nations such as Australia and the UK of the 1990s. Moreover, by juxtaposing first-order inequities such as gender and 'race' with individualising discourses of 'personality' and 'lifestyle', such texts potentially warded off criticism that structural inequities may be being overlooked. In addition, the implicit suggestion that diversity extends beyond collective inequities to individuals of gender, 'race' or class suggested that all (white, majority ethnic)

---

[18] Heidi Safia Mirza, 'Race, Gender and Educational Desire' (inaugural professorial lecture, Middlesex University, UK, 2005). http://www.mdx.ac.uk/hssc/research/cres.htm (accessed July, 2006).

[19] Ibid., 15–16.

[20] R. Roosevelt Thomas, *Beyond Race and Gender: Unleashing the Power of Your Total Workforce by Unleashing Diversity* (New York: AMACOM, 1991).

[21] Deborah Jones, Judith Pringle, and Deborah Shepherd, '"Managing Diversity" Meets Aotearoa/ New Zealand', *Personnel Review* 29, no. 3 (2000): 364–80.

[22] Ibid., 368.

[23] Thomas, *Beyond Race and* Gender, 12, cited in Jones, Pringle, and Shepherd, '"Managing Diversity"', 368.

men were diverse too and needed to be considered in diversity policies. However, as critical feminist and postcolonial scholars have noted, beneath the surface of these consensual artefacts, asymmetrical power relations of gender and 'race' remain unresolved.[24] Instead, as Mirza asserts, they may surface surreptitiously through, for example, the emergence of new terminology such as 'cultural differences' when employed in education debates.

A major concern of key texts such as *Beyond Race and Gender* is that when difference is decontextualised from historically and economically situated power struggles located in axes of gender, 'race', socio-economic status and other forms of inequality, it becomes a form of 'benign variation (diversity), for instance, rather than … conflict, struggle or threat to disruption'. In so doing, it '"bypasses power as well as history to suggest a harmonious, empty pluralism"'[25] which may indeed be more harmful than helpful for equity groups. Who benefits from such a reading of diversity and who loses out? For example, in relation to educational leadership, current figures in England would suggest that women, and in particular those of black and ethnic minority origin, remain disproportionately under-represented within formal positions of authority in schools[26] and universities.[27] This is despite the prevalence of 'diversity talk' in English universities and a range of government action plans and policies.[28] Secondly, in performative times, when education is positioned as an economic product to be managed, consumed and delivered, emptied of genuine commitment to equity issues, such rhetoric may become a substitute for real and significant action on the equity front. Indeed, it has been argued that such 'institutional "speech acts" … "work precisely by *not* bringing about the effects they name"'. Hence, the danger is that 'having a good race equality policy gets translated into *being good at race equality* – "as if saying is doing"'.[29]

Drawing on the preceding discourses as well as recent mapping of diversity in the educational leadership field, let us now turn to an examination of recent scholarship in order to explore the material consequences for educational leadership scholarship and practice in regard to the take-up of these varying approaches to diversity.

Diversity as the object or subject of educational leadership?

A quick glance across current journals, books and studies in educational administration reveals a developing concern around issues of diversity and educational leadership.[30] A

---

[24]Jones, Pringle, and Shepherd, '"Managing Diversity"'.

[25]C.T. Mohanty, 'On Race and Voice: Challenges for Liberal Education in the 1990s', in *Beyond a Dream Deferred: Multicultural Education and the Politics of Excellence*, ed. B. Thompson and S. Tyagi (Minnesota: University of Minnesota Press, 1993), 42, cited in Heidi Safia Mirza, 'The In/visible Journey: Black Women's Life-long Lessons in Higher Education', in *Gender and Lifelong Learning*, ed. C. Leathwood and B. Francis (London: Routledge, 2006), 213.

[26]Olwen McNamara, Helen Gunter, Zeynep Onat-Stelma, John Howson, and Almut Sprigade, 'Women Teachers' Careers' (paper presented at the annual British Educational Research Association (BERA) conference, London, September 5–9, 2007).

[27]Mirza, 'The In/visible Journey', 207, 218, 232.

[28]Ibid., 216.

[29]Sarah Ahmed, 'The Non-performativity of Anti-racism' (paper presented at the State University of New York, New York, April 6, 2005), cited in Mirza, 'The In/visible Journey', 217.

[30]For example, Clive Dimmock and Allan Walker, *Educational Leadership: Culture and Diversity* (London: Sage, 2005); Helen Gunter, 'Educational Leadership and the Challenge of Diversity', *Educational Management Administration and Leadership* 34, no. 2 (2006): 257–68; Lumby with Coleman, *Leadership and Diversity*; Jane Wilkinson, 'Policy and Leadership as Practice: Senior Women Academics and the "Risky Business" of Diversity Policies in Enterprise Universities' (paper presented at the Australian Association of Research in Education, Fremantle, Australia, November 25–29, 2007).

rising interest in related areas such as cross-cultural comparative approaches to school leadership is also apparent.[31] Despite this flourishing of inquiry, however, there remains a relative dearth of empirical studies in the area of diversity and educational leadership, especially in regard to formal educational leaders such as principals/head teachers. Moreover, it has been argued that in terms of issues around diversity and social justice, there is both a 'paucity in forward-looking critical theory and practice to develop … engagement', and involvement at a rhetorical level only.[32] A number of reasons may be responsible for this state of affairs. One may be the way in which leadership paradigms of (Anglocentric and often gendered and classed) whiteness continue to be the taken-for-granted norm underlying most studies of educational administration in nations such as Australia and England.[33] Minority ethnicity tends to remain the property of the managed (non-white, non-male) 'others' such as students or staff. Given the increase in ethnically diverse student populations within schools, and the belated embracing of some aspects of diversity in educational administration scholarship,[34] now would seem to be an opportune time to examine recent empirical work within the field, and suggest existing strengths, gaps and areas for future research.

Two recent articles (2007) from *International Studies in Educational Administration* were selected.[35] They were chosen as they illustrated how the deployment of different discourses of diversity, when applied to a study of formal leadership within schools with ethnically diverse populations, can have very different effects in terms of theory and leadership practices. The journal is produced by the Commonwealth Council for Educational Administration and Management (CCEAM) whose member countries include nations as diverse as Namibia, Cyprus and the UK. Hence, its articles may challenge essentialising and homogenising paradigms of educational leadership which draw almost exclusively on perspectives taken from Western literature and practice.[36] The two texts examined the leadership of ethnically diverse schools largely from the principals' perspective, with empirical data based on research in Norway, New Zealand, Canada and Australia. In both articles, principals were the main focus of the study. For ease of reference, the articles will be referred to by their authors' names.

In analysing the articles, I adopted critical discourse analysis as method and methodology through an examination of both dominant and submerged discourses and silences and gaps around diversity and educational leadership. Critical discourse analysis is based on the premise that both 'discourse and language in everyday life may function ideologically … to make asymmetrical relations of power and particular textual portrayals of social and biological worlds appear given, commonsensical, and "natural"'.[37]

---

[31]Allan Walker and Clive Dimmock, eds., *School Leadership and Administration: Adopting a Cultural Perspective* (New York: RoutledgeFalmer, 2002).

[32]Morrison, Lumby, and Sood, 'Diversity and Diversity Management', 277.

[33]Jane Wilkinson, 'But What Do We Know About Women? Feminist Scholarship for/about Women Academic Leaders', *New Zealand Journal of Educational Leadership* 22 (2007), no. 2: 13–21.

[34]Morrison, Lumby, and Sood, 'Diversity and Diversity Management', 277.

[35]Jennie Billott, J. Tim Goddard, and Neil Cranston, 'How Principals Manage Ethnocultural Diversity: Learnings from Three Countries', *International Studies in Educational Administration* 35, no. 2 (2007); Gunn Vedoy and Jorunn Moller, 'Successful School Leadership for Diversity? Examining Two Contrasting Examples of Working for Democracy in Norway', *International Studies in Educational Administration* 35, no. 3 (2007).

[36]Alan Walker and John Walker, 'Challenging the Boundaries of Sameness: Leadership Through the Valuing of Difference', *Journal of Educational Administration* 36, no. 1 (1998): 12.

[37]Allen Luke, 'Critical Discourse Analysis', in *International Encyclopedia of the Sociology of Education*, ed. Lawrence J. Saha, vol. 1 (Oxford: Pergamon, 1997), 54.

Using a critical approach to diversity, I analysed how the term diversity was defined, applied and theorised in the articles. The crucial point is that if theory and practice in regard to approaches to diversity and educational leadership is to be reinvigorated,[38] it is this kind of questioning with which the field will need to seriously engage.

The case of the missing 'p' words? Power and politics in studies of diversity and educational leadership

'How Principals Manage Ethnocultural Diversity: Learnings from Three Countries' by Jennie Billot, Tim Goddard, and Neil Cranston, is a comparative study of how principals in Australia, New Zealand and Canada managed schools with large numbers of culturally diverse students.[39] The term 'ethnocultural' was initially defined in the text as encompassing a multiplicity of areas including 'language, socio-economic status, "race", ethnicity, culture, heritage, gender and sexual orientiation'.[40] Most commonly, however, the phrase was mainly deployed in the article by the Australian and New Zealand principals as a synonym for ethnic diversity, and in particular, that which was 'different' from a largely unexamined Anglocentric norm of whiteness within leadership. Notably, the Canadian principals emphasised the more 'inclusive nature of the concept'.[41]

The data provided in the article suggested that the principals mainly drew upon a managing-for-diversity discourse, that is, (minority ethnic) diversity was seen as an asset within the schools that leaders heralded.[42] Principals focused positively upon minority ethnic students in terms of their cultural differences but this difference was largely measured from an unstated majority ethnic norm. This was signified by the repetition of active verbs such as 'manage', 'acknowledge', 'value', integrate', 'celebrate' and nouns such as 'tolerance' when discussing the various principals' approaches to ethnocultural diversity. They commented that '"one of the strengths of the school … is the degree of tolerance here from an ethnic point of view"'; another observed that she '"saw the diversity in her school adding to the school's rich culture"'.[43] Interestingly, the Australian and New Zealand emphasis upon celebration and acknowledgement of difference was less marked in the Canadian context. The latter group 'felt that celebrating the three F's of multiculturalism – food, festivals and folk dancing – did not really allow the development of a deep understanding of "other" in relation to dominant society'.[44]

The preceding comment of the Canadian administrators points to a potential danger of the managing-for-diversity discourse. Its underlying emphasis is upon a pluralistic approach to culture and education in which the fundamental right of minority ethnic groups to keep their home culture, language and that which differentiates them from the majority culture, is asserted. A pluralistic focus upon pedagogical approaches, practices and curriculum is a major advance from conservative, assimilationist and monocultural approaches to education.[45] However, the inherent danger of a surface emphasis upon culture such as the 'three F's' may undercut its good intentions. It signals a major criticism of the pluralistic approach, that is, how 'power relations between majority and minorities' are ignored, and

---

[38]Morrison, Lumby, and Sood, 'Diversity and Diversity Management', 277.
[39]Billot, Goddard, and Cranston, 'How Principals Manage', 3.
[40]Ibid., 4.
[41]Ibid., 10.
[42]Blackmore, 'Deconstructing Diversity Discourses', 189.
[43]Billot, Goddard, and Cranston, 'How Principals Manage', 9–11.
[44]Ibid., 14.
[45]Vedoy and Moller, 'Successful School Leadership', 60.

'actions taken … (in education) … could be understood as compensatory'.[46] What forms of knowledge about leadership as a construct and practice are produced by this discourse?

The use of verbs such as 'manage' and 'value' connotes a set of asymmetrical power relations between the agents who do the 'managing/valuing' (in this case, the principals whose ethnicity is unspecified) and the objects of celebration and tolerance (that is, 'ethnoculturally diverse' and thus very possibly non-Anglo, non-white students). Indeed, the title of the article itself, 'How Principals Manage Ethnocultural Diversity: Learnings from Three Countries' grammatically places the reader's focus upon the subject of the verb 'manage', that is, the apparently ethnically and gender neutral subject (principals) who manage the objects in their care, that is, students of non-white origin. Through the use of active verbs such as 'celebrate', 'manage' and 'tolerate', the principals are positioned as agentic subjects who possess the formal (white) authority to tolerate or acknowledge (non-white) students. Thus the implicit threat is that they also have the authority to withdraw this 'tolerance' at any time.

The respect for minority ethnic groups' cultures which the principals reveal within the text is a plus whose importance cannot be overemphasised. However, as Ghassan Hage notes in his critique of Australian multicultural policies, 'racism and tolerant multiculturalism are two sides of the one coin, two manifestations of the entitlement which only Anglo-Celts claim, to speak'.[47] This is not to suggest that the principals are racist and indeed the opposite is true. However, what Hage's quotation is signalling is that in Australian policy texts and discourses such as multiculturalism, there is an unintended paternalistic subject position carved out when the whiteness of the normative centre which does the tolerating is taken-for-granted and naturalised. It is this unexamined sense of white entitlement to tolerate the (non-white) ethnic 'otherness' of the students which underpins the constructions of diversity and leadership within the article. It positions students from non-Anglo origin as the passive recipients of middle, white leadership largesse. Ethnic diversity remains a property of these 'others' whereas the white authority, which underpins leadership legitimacy, remains unexamined. Within the article, the lack of problematisation of the political implications which underpin the managing-for-diversity discourse that many of the principals draw upon, means that knowledge and practices in regard to leadership for/about ethnoculturally diverse schools remain fixed and unchallenged in a white, ethnocentrically framed paradigm of leadership.

The second article, 'Successful School Leadership for Diversity? Examining Two Contrasting Examples of Working for Democracy in Norway' by Gunn Vedoy and Jorunn Moller,[48] explores two culturally diverse schools in Norway known for their success in multicultural education. The authors utilise a critical discourse analysis of the contrasting, dominant discourses which the two principals call upon in order to explain their 'beliefs, attitudes, and focus' in terms of their 'impact on … education for diversity'.[49] The text defines diversity as (non-Norwegian) ethnicity, that is, referring to students who have immigrated from other countries and who 'for a shorter or longer period need personalized instruction in the Norwegian language'.[50] The article is explicit about both its theoretical lens, that is, critical multiculturalism and its method, critical discourse analysis. It explains

---

[46] James Ryan, *Leading Diverse Schools* (Dordrecht: Kluwer Academic Publishers, 2006), cited in Vedoy and Moller, 'Successful School Leadership', 60.

[47] Ghassan Hage, *White Nation: Fantasies of White Supremacy in a Multicultural Society* (Sydney: Pluto Press, 1998), cited in Susan Sheridan, 'The "Australian Woman" and Her Migrant Others in the Postwar Australian Women's Weekly', *Continuum* 14, no. 2 (2000): 130.

[48] Vedoy and Moller, 'Successful School Leadership'.

[49] Ibid., 61.

[50] Ibid., 59.

that the former has 'its roots in theories of social justice, and examines institutions that exist for the common good'.[51] It notes that a core objective of critical multiculturalism in schools includes making the 'majority's culture and the pedagogy ... explicit' but importantly, not as an 'objective of assimilation'.[52] It also notes the influence upon diversity education of a major educational policy which emphasises the importance of both 'democracy and diversity' in the Norwegian system. The authors observe that the nation's 'strong commitment to comprehensive education and social justice' is underpinned by 'social democratic politics for promoting equity'.[53] A more transformative diversity discourse, that is, leadership and management practices which clearly articulate social justice values founded in democratic principles and which foster agency,[54] is implied by the authors. It is manifested through the article's explicit examination of how the principals' differing discourses about diversity result in a range of contrasting forms of leadership knowledge and practice. These include areas such as pedagogical approaches, expectation setting for students, staff and student relationship, openness to dissent and the general democratic atmosphere within the two schools. The article is clear from the outset in regard to its adoption of a critical discursive approach to method and theory, which assists in making explicit the constructions of power and knowledge production which underly its examination of differing educational leadership approaches to diversity.

For example, in their analysis of the differing discourses of the 'Brage' and 'Skog' principals, the writers note that 'respect' is the dominant discourse of the Brage principal, whereas the Skog principal emphasises 'caring'. The former discourse has much in common with critical multiculturalism, whereas the latter discourse is very similar to pluralism.[55] As the authors observe, it has been argued that both perspectives are needed for responsive education in ethnically diverse societies.[56] However, there are a number of clear material consequences for the leadership, organisation, students and staff in both schools as a result of the adoption of these differing discourses. For example, they assert that the Brage School principal's focus on 'high expectations for minority students' language needs…', a 'clearly formulated' and 'accessible' pedagogy and an emphasis upon 'teachers' professonalism',[57] is translated into a highly visible leadership style in which he knows all the students well and they, him.[58] They contend that there is a clear formulation of student learning embedded in 'educational theory ... associated to the public sphere'; great clarity in his desires for the school, but crucially an atmosphere of openness to disagreement for 'all topics are opens up [sic] for professional discussions'.[59] Also observed is a deliberate strategy to achieve heterogeneity amongst the staff in terms of gender and ethnic diversity; as well as clear formal responsibilities for staff in terms of co-operation in regard to the students' education (for example, education of the minority ethnic students is seen as the responsibility of all staff and not just the Norwegian language specialist teachers). In terms of students, teachers and the principal, a sense of agency is noted through the observation that in the school there exists a 'relation of equality where all individuals act and speak on equal terms'.[60]

---

[51]Ibid., 60.
[52]Ibid.
[53]Ibid., 58.
[54]Blackmore, 'Deconstructing Diversity Discourses', 192–3.
[55]Vedoy and Moller, 'Successful School Leadership', 62.
[56]Ibid., 63.
[57]Ibid., 62.
[58]Ibid.
[59]Ibid., 64.
[60]Ibid., 63–5.

In contrast, the authors contend that the Brage School principal's focus upon caring for students places the latter group in an asymmetrical set of power relations to the staff and principal.[61] The authors note that the principal's 'emphasis on understanding and caring without clear educational goals is politically disputed' (by professional staff). Moreover, by emphasising the 'difference in students' home culture' as the key means for comprehending the student population, rather than in relation to pedagogical theories, a deficit model of student difference is propounded.[62] The staff, they observe, is homogenous, with the majority being older females and the principal is far less visible to students. Despite excellent systems and goals for learning, 'staff is pulling in opposite directions, with some teachers choosing to focus upon students' deficits'.[63] In terms of power, the writers argue that the 'focus on caring leads into a discourse of goodness, which, in turn, disarms those who might want to disagree openly'. In turn, this leads to difficulties in realising collective decisions due to the lack of openness in regard to conflict.[64] Hence, despite the best of intentions and programmes, the researchers contend that an asymmetrical status quo is preserved between staff and principals, on the one hand, and students on the other.[65] In conclusion, Vedoy and Moller argue that in terms of a genuine working towards social justice, inclusive, democratic leadership practices and potentially, better student outcomes, a 'caring approach through a focus on … [student] … possibilities and respect, not on deficit, is crucial'.[66]

Pulling the threads together

The aim of this brief textual analysis of the two articles is not to 'name and shame' specific scholarship in this area, nor to necessarily privilege one diversity discourse or methodological approach over another. Indeed, both pluralistic and critical multicultural approaches are integral aspects of educative work in ethnically diverse societies.[67] So too is the application of a range of critical methods and methodological tools to scholarship in this area. Both texts make a clear contribution to emergent work in an area of major importance for educational leadership in these globalising times. This is particularly the case in terms of providing much-needed empirical data and analysis to begin to decipher the 'black box' of diversity and leadership in schools with high numbers of students from minority ethnic and Indigenous origins. Equally important is research into leadership of monoculturally Anglocentric schools so that the implicit privileging of whiteness as a form of ethnicity can be explored, including its intersection with other axes of difference such as gender and class.

Rather the aim of the analysis is to point to the highly political and contested nature of diversity and educational leadership as an emergent field within the broader scholarship. As a recent text notes, 'There is no safe ground anywhere in discussing diversity, no agreement on any aspect, not even that diversity is an issue at all, let alone how one should act in response'.[68] The latter point, however, is not an excuse to ignore the area, dismiss its

[61]Ibid., 63.
[62]Ibid.
[63]Ibid., 63–4.
[64]Ibid., 64.
[65]Ibid.
[66]Ibid., 65.
[67]Stephen Castles, 'Migration, Citizenship, and Education', in *Diversity and Citizenship Education: Global Perspectives*, ed. J. Banks (San Francisco: Jossey-Bass, 2005), 17–48, cited in Vedoy and Moller, 'Successful School Leadership', 62–3.
[68]Lumby with Coleman, *Leadership and Diversity*, 12.

importance or turn our respective gaze from it for fear of the exotic 'otherness' of theorising in this area.[69] Instead, it is to stress three recommendations in terms of future directions for scholarship in this emergent field. The first is the importance of a serious engagement by educational leadership scholars with critical theory. Fields such as feminist, black, Indigenous and postcolonial scholarship have had, of necessity, to grapple in ongoing ways with the thorny issues of theory and practice in relation to identity and difference. Critical theory in organisational management, emerging work with critical feminist leadership, and critical masculinities, are other productive bodies for exploration. The insights, struggles and points of contest from these approaches reveal crucial learnings and subjugated knowledges about leadership, which have begun to challenge mainstream bodies of knowledge in this area. They can provide scholars with rich insights into their application for our work, as Vedoy and Moller's article reveals.

Secondly, it is a plea for scholastic self-reflexivity, in particular in terms of explicitly theorising and foregrounding notions of power, through the examination and interrogation of taken-for-granted constructs that underlie empirical data. Otherwise, social justice intentions are severely undercut because of the utilisation of discourses, which unwittingly perpetuate an inequitable status quo. Again Vedoy and Moller's article exposes this danger through its critical analysis of the concrete implications for practice that flow from one principal's adoption of a caring discourse in regard to students.

The third point follows from the second. In order to achieve such self-reflexivity, the use of a range of 'critical thinking tools' as method and methodology,[70] be it critical discourse analysis, or those drawn from other bodies of scholarship such as philosophy and the Social Sciences, can assist in not only '"theoris(ing) … about our privilege, but also … tak(ing)… stock of our much vaunted reflexivity as well"'.[71] Such tools can provide valuable frameworks for analysis of data, for they assist in interrogating and illuminating the 'common sense' of much educational leadership research.

Conclusion

In making the preceding suggestions, I recognise that attempts to transform current leadership practices on the grounds of equity and diversity are deeply threatening to the status quo and may frequently be met with passive resistance or outright hostility. However, these kinds of reactions do not explain why so frequently scholarship in the field of educational administration overlooks the implications of diversity in regard to leadership composition and practice. This is where critical black and Indigenous feminist research, along with other forms of critical scholarship, can play an important role in revealing educational leadership and diversity as intensely political and social. Theorising about power allows us to examine leadership for diversity discourses and practices as a set of processes rather than a given.[72] Such critical tools can provide scholars and administrators with the resources to not only

[69]Helen Gunter, 'Comparing and Contrasting Perspectives: Mapping the Field of Educational Leadership', in *Rethinking Educational Leadership*, ed. N. Bennett and L. Anderson (London: Sage, 2003), 190, cited in Morrison, Lumby, and Sood, 'Diversity and Diversity Management', 282.
[70]Loic J.D. Wacquant, 'Towards a Reflexive Sociology: A Workshop with Pierre Bourdieu', *Sociology Theory* 7, no. 1 (1989): 50.
[71]J. Cavanaugh, '(In)corporating the Other? Managing the Politics of Workplace Difference', in *Managing the Organisational Melting Pot. Dilemmas of Workplace Diversity*, ed. P. Prasad, A. Mills, M. Elmes, and A. Prasad (Thousand Oaks, CA: Sage, 1997), 47, cited in Blackmore, 'Deconstructing Diversity Discourses', 192.
[72]Helen Gunter, *Leading Teachers* (London: Continuum International Publishing Group, 2005), 6.

answer back to individualising, socially inequitable and divisive diversity claims, but to actively intervene in order to produce genuinely productive, democratic and socially inclusive ways of leading.

Acknowledgements

The author wishes to thank Professor Jill Blackmore of Deakin University, for it was in discussions with her that the idea for this article originated. Thank you also to Professors Helen Gunter and Peter Gronn, as well as the two anonymous reviewers, for valuable feedback on earlier drafts of the article.

The continuing politics of mistrust: performance management and the erosion of professional work

Tanya Fitzgerald

Introduction

We live in dangerous times. The opening decade of the twenty-first century has been marked by increasing concern about public safety that has erupted over the emergence of a number of threats. This includes, but is not limited to, the threat posed by terrorism, the threat of political interference and the waging of war in countries seemingly disconnected from democracy and democratic processes, the threat of ecological and biological disasters such as global warming and the avian flu epidemic and, more recently, the threat of economic collapse due to volatile markets, fluctuating currencies and decreasing supplies of natural resources. Yet, in subtle and logical ways, the apparent 'commonsense' formulation of responses to these threats has become legitimised and normalised in our everyday lives and practices.[1]

Schools, as institutions of the State, are similarly under threat and face unprecedented challenges. There has been a gradual yet insistent erosion of trust in teachers and their professional knowledge, autonomy and expertise. One of the new and emerging threats is the mistrust of the professions and professionals (this includes the teaching, medical and legal professions) and the consequent public certainty that the imposition of standards, targets, and accountability is the antidote.[2] This has resulted in a bifurcated public policy response that

---

[1]See Michael W. Apple, *Educating the 'Right' Way: Markets, Standards, God and Inequality* (New York: RoutledgeFalmer, 2001) for a persuasive argument on the conservative right and the impact of the call for a return to a 'common' past and 'commonsense approaches'.

[2]The historical and contemporary underpinning of calls for quality, standards and the audit regime is well covered by Apple, *Educating the 'Right' Way.*

has involved, in the first stage, the restructuring of schools and, in the second stage, the restructuring of the professions and professional work. And as the educational reform agenda of the late 1980s and 1990s in New Zealand and elsewhere demonstrated, teachers' compliance is critical to ensure the delivery of this 'new' and 'improved' agenda.[3] One of the ways to secure a level of direct and immediate commitment by teachers is via performance management policies and processes that describe and prescribe what ought to occur in schools (at an organisational level), in staff rooms (at a professional level) and in classrooms (at a pedagogical level). As this article argues, performance management, articulated and framed as one of the policy solutions to the espoused 'problem' of schools and teachers, has not alleviated mistrust but has intensified scrutiny and, as a result, sharpened this mistrust.

The first stage of these politics of mistrust was embedded in the radical restructuring of schools that occurred in New Zealand in the closing decades of the twentieth century.[4] These reforms were premised on the assumption that schools had to become more fiscally efficient and effective. Although there was an implicit level of trust in schools, teachers and their communities in the devolved model of school self-management, in reality the continuing nature of centralised control has emphasised that neither schools nor teachers, at either an individual or collective level, can be trusted.

The State, however, could not be assured that teachers were be trusted to implement the reform agenda, a level of surveillance and *public* regulation was required to ensure that they were acting in expected ways. Hence, the evolution of agencies in New Zealand such as the Education Review Office (ERO) and the Teachers Council to define, regulate, audit, and sanction schools and teachers if they do not meet insistent requirements that are enshrined in policies that prescribe what teachers should and ought to accomplish. In other words, schools and teachers were identified as a policy problem and could not be trusted to exercise professional judgement and act in professional ways (and this includes professional accountability). Thus, public accountability replaced *professional* accountability and autonomy.[5]

The second stage of these politics of mistrust originated from public dissatisfaction with the teaching profession that provided 'evidence' that policy makers required in order to affect a policy solution.[6] In response to these demands for public accountability, ongoing and concurrent performance management policies were systematically introduced to assess, evaluate, regulate and monitor teachers. One of the consequences of these regimes of performance management is that teachers, particularly those with labels such as 'senior manager' or 'middle manager',[7] are required to act for and on behalf of the State as well as

---

[3]Alex Moore, Gwyn Edwards, David Halpin, and Rosalyn George, 'Compliance, Resistance and Pragmatism: The (Re) Construction of Schoolteacher Identities in a Period of Intensive Education Reform', *British Educational Research Journal* 28, no. 4 (2002): 551–65.

[4]I have argued this point in considerable detail elsewhere. See Tanya Fitzgerald, 'Remodelling Schools and Schooling, Teachers and Teaching', in *Modernising Schools: People, Learning and Organisations*, ed. Graham Butt, Helen M. Gunter, and Hywel Thomas (London: Continuum, 2007), 163–75.

[5]See here Tanya Fitzgerald, Howard Youngs, and Peter Grootenboer, 'Bureaucratic Control or Professional Autonomy: Performance Management in NZ Schools', *School Leadership and Management* 23, no. 1 (2003): 91–105.

[6]Philip Capper and Rae Munro, 'Professionals or Workers?: Changing Teachers Conditions of Service', in *New Zealand Education Policy Today*, ed. Sue Middleton, John Codd, and Alison Jones (Wellington: Allen & Unwin, 1990); Edward Fiske and Helen Ladd, *When Schools Compete: A Cautionary Tale* (Washington, DC: Brookings Institution Press, 2000).

[7]These terms are used in New Zealand schools although there is a gradual shift away from 'manager' and 'management' to 'leader (for example middle leader) and leadership (for example the Senior Leadership team).

engage in multiple policy directives such as compulsory teacher registration, attestation and annual appraisals that determine what 'counts' as a good teacher. Not only then has the professional work of teachers intensified,[8] what 'counts' as a good teacher and good teaching has shifted from the profession to the managerial apparatus of the State (and this includes not only performance management policies but also those agencies which audit and report on the performance of teachers and schools). The shift in accountability from the profession to policy makers has imposed an audit culture[9] that describes and prescribes what ought to occur in schools, staffrooms, and classrooms. Performance management is, I would argue, no less than a direct assault on the teaching profession and teachers as professionals. Indeed, there can be little doubt, the restructuring of schools and teaching has irrevocably changed the content and purposes of public education.[10]

In this article I firstly present an abbreviated history of the introduction of performance management in New Zealand against a backdrop of alleged concerns about teachers and teaching to surface an understanding of ways in which these policies continue to erode and corrode trust in teachers and their professional work. More specifically, I argue that the decreasing professional autonomy experienced by teachers about their work and pedagogic practices over the past two decades is situated in a period in which there was, and continues to be, increasing control by the State not only about what is taught but who can teach and under what conditions. The net effect of this decline in professional autonomy has been a marked shift from self-regulation to mandated regulation that has led to teachers becoming 'a technical workforce to be managed and controlled rather than a profession to be respected'.[11] Thus, as illustrated by the New Zealand example, there has been a progressive yet unrelenting erosion of trust in the professional work of teachers. This shift has been accompanied by policy solutions that initially located schools as the 'problem', to the identification of teachers as the 'problem' to be remedied through performance management policies and practices. The increasing audit of teachers' performance could assure the State and its agencies that teachers' commitment to the seemingly 'new' and 'modern' practices of the self-managed school has been secured. Performance management has irrevocably fostered a counter-productive culture of mistrust that has simultaneously intensified and de-professionalised the professional work of teachers.

An abbreviated overview

In the past two decades, terms such as performance, standards, outputs, targets, accountability, choice, quality, improvement, and efficiency have littered the language of education policy and practice in New Zealand as well as elsewhere.[12] In various and diverse fields such as education, health, public services and agencies (namely the police, fire department, local government) as well as consumer services (for example trains, buses, planes, and supermarket checkouts), 'standards' of service and delivery are publicly audited, collated and the information disseminated, presumably because it is deemed to be 'in the public interest'.[13]

[8]This point has been well argued by John A. Codd, 'Educational Reform, Accountability and the Culture of Distrust', *New Zealand Journal of Educational Studies* 34, no. 1 (1999): 45–53.
[9]See here the work of Michael Power, *The Audit Explosion* (London: Demos, 1994).
[10]Codd, 'Educational Reform'; David Hartley, 'Marketing and the Re-enactment of School Management', *British Journal of Sociology of Education* 20, no. 3 (1999): 309–23.
[11]Sally Tomlinson, *Education in a Post-welfare Society* (Buckingham, UK: Open University Press, 2001), 36.
[12]Fitzgerald, 'Remodelling Schools'.
[13]Apple, *Educating the 'Right' Way.*

From displays in places such as MacDonald's 'Employee of the Month' awards ostensibly for service and meeting standards of delivery, to school audit reports on websites such as the Office for Standards in Education (OfSTED) in England or the ERO in New Zealand, to public lists on railway station walls in England that 'name and shame' those who failed to purchase a rail ticket, our everyday lives are recorded, audited and made public. Whether a teacher, train traveller, or school, harsh sanctions are imposed on those who do not conform to pre-ordained rules and regulations.[14] To ensure that standards are met, performance is constantly monitored and reported, and supervisors or managers are afforded responsibility for both workers and their work. I wonder then how long it will take before classroom activities are recorded just as telephone conversations are taped for ubiquitous reasons such as 'training' or 'quality' when contact is made with internet service providers, banks, insurance companies, or utility suppliers?

These forms of management practices are not new and have been an integral aspect of the way in which schools and teachers have been managed since the late 1980s. Performance management, an evaluative system ostensibly designed to standardise, regulate and control professional work, is not a 'modern' technique to control and define teachers and their work. As I have commented elsewhere, the inspection and examination of teachers in New Zealand can be traced to the introduction of compulsory schooling in 1877.[15] Across 111 years, the performance of teachers was scrutinised by inspectors who were appointed under the aegis of regional boards of education. Notably, this level of inspection graded teachers but at the same time provided a mechanism of support for teachers and schools. This level of professional trust and autonomy could not, however, withstand the intense ambush that the neo-liberal reforms in the closing decade of the twentieth century delivered.

The educational reforms of 1989 were predicated on neo-liberal ideology that dictated the need for schools to adopt the tenets of business management practices and become fiscally efficient and effective business units.[16] Hence, both accountability and responsibility for the performance of schools and teachers were re-distributed to the local level and therefore provided the policy apparatus for schools and teachers to be 'named and shamed' if they failed to meet the required standards. The adoption of the structures and discourses of new public management without doubt delivered organisational efficiencies and, consequently, the introduction of mission statements, vision and values, strategic plans, marketing initiatives, and the auditing of teacher and school performance have reinforced the apparent rationality of structures and hierarchies.[17] In New Zealand schools, performance management, professional development, competency and teacher registration are inextricably linked. On the one hand, the meshing of such systems could be expedient, on the other, this apparent

---

[14]Jill Blackmore and Pat Thomson, 'Just "Good and Bad News"? Disciplinary Imaginaries of Head Teachers in Australian and English Print Media', *Journal of Education Policy* 19, no. 3 (2004): 301–20.

[15]Tanya Fitzgerald, 'Potential Paradoxes in Performance Appraisal: Emerging Issues for New Zealand Schools', in *Managing Teacher Appraisal and Performance: A Comparative Approach*, ed. David Middlewood and Carol Cardno (London: RoutledgeFalmer Press, 2001), 112–24.

[16]Fiske and Ladd, *When Schools Compete.*

[17]The effect of business management practices in New Zealand schools is highlighted by John Codd, 'Teachers as "Managed Professionals" in the Global Education Industry: The New Zealand Experience', *Educational Review* 57, no. 2 (2005): 193–206; Marian Court, 'Talking Back to New Public Management Versions of Accountability in Education', *Educational Management Administration & Leadership* 32, no. 2 (2004): 171–94. For a discussion on new public management see Jonathon Boston, John Martin, June Pallot, and Pat Walsh, *Public Management: The New Zealand Model* (Auckland: Oxford University Press, 1996).

commonsense approach provides a mechanism for the introduction of performance-related pay.[18] Significantly, while teachers recognise that some form of professional accountability and responsibility is a core aspect of their work as *professionals*, teachers and their unions in New Zealand have, to date, resisted performance-related pay.[19]

Since 1997, schools have been required to introduce performance management systems and personnel policies to promote and sustain high levels of staff performance.[20] The primary purpose of performance management was to provide 'a positive framework for improving the quality of teaching and learning' and that performance management systems were designed to be 'flexible', 'appropriate' within a 'minimum quality assurance and accountability framework'.[21] A direct consequence of this espoused belief was that appraisers would act as neutral agents of policy. Thus, teachers enacted policy directives in their role as either an appraiser or appraisee and were directly involved in managerial processes with their professional colleagues such as the setting of annual objectives that were aligned with organisational strategies, classroom observation, and formal discussions with colleagues with regards their performance against set criteria.

Mahony and Hextall correctly assert that performance management is a 'process which links people and jobs to the strategy and objectives of the organisation'.[22] Hence, performance management systems ensure a direct connection between teachers' work and organisational success. This in turn presupposes that teaching and learning can be regulated and reduced to input–output models. It is further possible that performance could be accelerated in an optimal set of circumstances. By its very nature, performance management disconnects professional and pedagogic practices,[23] continues to de-professionalise teaching and teachers' work[24] and is the antithesis of what it means to be a professional and engage in professional work.

The year 1999 heralded the next level of audit and regulation with the introduction of the *Professional Standards* that further tightened control of teachers and their work. Articulated as 'part of the Government's strategy for developing and maintaining high-quality teaching and leadership in schools and improving learning outcomes for students',[25] these standards, with the by-line *Criteria for Quality Teaching*, described the key elements of teacher performance and provided 'a base for assessing teachers' progress in relation to pay

---

[18]Although 'successful' attestation means an increase to the next salary level, there is not at present an overt system whereby teachers receive bonus payments for their work. However, what is less known is that principals in New Zealand schools received salary increments based on their implementation of performance management systems. As performance management was not optional, the payment of this additional money appears to be incongruous.

[19]See Fitzgerald, 'Potential Paradoxes' and Fitzgerald, Youngs, and Grootenboer, 'Bureaucratic Control'. The impossibility of meshing performance management and performance-related pay in the New Zealand context is also the subject of John O'Neill, ed., *Teacher Appraisal in New Zealand: Beyond the Impossible Triangle* (Palmerston North: ERDC Press, 1997).

[20]Ministry of Education, *Performance Management Systems* (Wellington: Learning Media, 1997).

[21]Ibid., 1.

[22]Pat Mahony and Ian Hextall, 'Performing and Conforming', in *The Performing School*, ed. Dennis Gleeson and Chris Husbands (London: RoutledgeFalmer, 2000), 177.

[23]This point is also well argues by Andy Hargreaves, *Changing Teachers, Changing Times: Teachers' Work and Culture in the Post Modern Age* (London: Cassell, 1994); Mike Bottery, 'The Challenge to Professionals from the New Public Management', *Oxford Review of Education* 22 (1996): 179–97.

[24]Fitzgerald, Youngs, and Grootenboer, 'Bureaucratic Control'; Fitzgerald, 'Remodelling Schools'.

[25]Ministry of Education, *Professional Standards: Criteria for Quality Teaching* (Wellington: Government Printer, 1999), 5.

progression, competency and professional development'.[26] In effect, both systems designed to assess the performance of teachers were aligned with organisational structures and managerial imperatives that were indicative of business management rather than educational practices. Labels such as 'leader', 'manager', 'appraiser', 'appraisee' were used to denote and reinforce formal relationships between teachers.[27] And while this produced a 'managed' system and teachers as 'managed' professionals as Codd has commented, the long-term effect of these neo-liberal policies has been the erosion of professional work, knowledge and expertise.[28] In other words, the State, in its employment contract with teachers, can identify, define and specify what ought to be taught (and conversely what should not be taught[29]) and insist, through performance management practices, that these demands are acknowledged, implemented, and formally recorded.

In the past two decades of educational reform, systems to regulate and control the work of teachers have become both legitimised and normalised in schools, not just in New Zealand but in Australia, England and North America. I would argue that the silent message that is being, and has been, relayed is that teachers cannot be trusted and therefore, they too must be subject to mechanisms of audit and surveillance. Moreover, the legislative pen[30] has ensured that teachers have been reconstructed as the managers of reform and, more specifically, performance management has made certain that teachers conform to externally mandated performance measures and that they exercise a level of individual and professional self-control to achieve what is required. The hegemony of performance management is predicated not only on the potentiality of professional sanction but further presupposes that teachers are compliant and docile. Furthermore, the rhetoric of the 'professional' has been co-opted to ensure that systems designed to standardise, regulate and control professional work and activities reside *outside* of the auspices of professional bodies and association. At a surface level, performance management is seductive insofar as it provides the illusion of professional accountability. The accountability is, not to the profession, but to the State.

Performance management has delivered for self-managed schools the mechanism to align product (teaching and learning) with outcomes (student results and teacher performance). These policies of performance management require teachers to make judgements and monitor the performance of their professional colleagues. This is a new form of control in which the professional work of teachers is simultaneously de-professionalised via the regulation of performance and re-professionalised by placing responsibility for this managerial work on *other* teachers.[31] Thus, as Rose concludes, teachers act as neo-liberal professionals[32] working for and on behalf of the State. Notwithstanding this point, as a form of assurance that teachers are acting in appropriate and mandated ways, agencies such

---

[26]Ibid., 4.

[27]The formalisation of line management structures and practices in schools is commented on by Horace Bennett, 'One Drop of Blood: Teacher Appraisal Mark 2', *Teacher Development* 3, no. 3 (1999): 411–28.

[28]Codd, 'Teachers as "Managed Professionals"'; Fitzgerald, Youngs, and Grootenboer, 'Bureaucratic Control'.

[29]On this point see Apple, *Educating the 'Right' Way*; Michael W. Apple, *Official Knowledge* (New York: Routledge, 1993).

[30]See Government of New Zealand, *Tomorrow's Schools: The Reform of Education Administration in New Zealand* (Wellington: Government Printer, 1988). This was the policy document that underpinned the reform agenda.

[31]See here Fitzgerald, Youngs, and Grootenboer, 'Bureaucratic Control'.

[32]Nikolas Rose, *Governing the Soul: The Shaping of the Private Self* (London: Routledge, 1989).

as the ERO audit the performance management processes to appease their policy masters and mistresses that performance management systems are *actively* in place in schools.

Policy solutions such as performance management systems (and this includes registration, attestation for salary purposes and professional standards) have been introduced as a benign way in which to make judgements about teachers' performance. More worryingly, these policy solutions are part of a deliberate strategy by the State to re-gain control of schools and schooling, teachers and teaching through the use of performance indicators. In much the same way that the market calls for the commodification of products (and education is one such example), teachers' work has been reduced to measures that commodify what ought and should be accomplished. Consequently, there is, as Michael Fielding suggests, no sense of the collective in the individual pursuit of meeting goals and targets.[33]

In summary, in New Zealand teachers have been increasingly subjected to systems that *assess* whether they meet criteria for registration, *evaluated* against a set of professional standards to judge competence, *attested* for salary increments and *appraised* to review performance. Underpinning these bureaucratic attempts to control the teaching profession is the assumption that teachers cannot be trusted to implement the agenda of the State and therefore these management practices are justified as commonsense responses to the 'problem' teachers present. What remains unclear is the extent to which systems of compliance produce the type of results it anticipates and demands.

Performance and standards

The culture of performance that has been organised around notions of quality, outcomes, targets and improvement objectives has gained steady momentum since the late 1980s; although it has neither been a straightforward nor uncontested process. The culture of performance has been introduced and legitimated in schools through performance management systems that have defined, regulated, controlled and sanctioned the work of teachers. However, performance management is set against a backdrop of State concerns that teachers cannot be trusted and reductive assumptions that in order for schools, teachers and students to be 'successful', performance measures should and ought to be aligned with private market principles and practices.[34] What remains concerning is that performance management, as a hegemonic set of practices, is designed to determine 'quality' and 'standards' that contribute to 'improvements', and is, accordingly, positioned as a commonsense response.[35] Consequently, the mantra of accountability, audit, targets, outcomes, standards and measures of performance has been imposed on schools as a policy solution to the 'problem' of raising achievement and improving schools. Yet, adequate levels of resources have not been provided for schools despite unrelenting public demands for increased performance.

The introduction of performance management, and subsequent systems to attest and register teachers according to a pre-determined set of professional standards,[36] was not accidental. As Gunter[37] and others have argued, performance management was no less than a

---

[33]Michael Fielding, 'Leadership, Personalisation and High Performance Schooling: Naming the New Totalitarianism', *School Leadership and Management* 26, no. 4 (2002): 347–69.

[34]John Clarke and Janet Newman, *The Managerial State* (London: Sage, 1997) argue the connection between private market principles as an efficient way to raise and improve standards.

[35]Links between teachers' professional standards and narratives of quality assurance and improvement are outlined by Judith Sachs, 'Teacher Professional Standards: Controlling or Developing Teaching?', *Teachers and Teaching* 9, no. 2 (2002): 175–86.

[36]Ministry of Education, *Professional Standards.*

[37]Helen M. Gunter, *Leaders and Leadership in Education* (London: Paul Chapman, 2001).

strategy to ensure compliance with the reform agenda and that changes in organisational practice would occur within a limited time frame. Performance management was a managerial strategy that directly intervened, as was its intention, in ways in which schools were managed and led and was predicated on policy assumptions that it was possible to construct the 'good' teacher who would deliver certain predetermined outcomes.[38] The underpinning logic of performance management was that teachers could not be trusted to control and regulate their own profession and therefore the direct intervention of the State was required to ensure not only a level of public and transparent accountability by teachers for their work, but that those teachers who did not perform would be sanctioned, in much the same way as those who had not complied with performance measures in train stations, airports, fast food counters, and supermarket checkouts as I have already outlined.

A secondary advantage that systems of performance management offered was a direct assurance that teachers were performing and conforming to the reform objectives. Thus, it was, I would suggest, critical for a strong State to be able to define, regulate and control teachers and teaching. Performance management was the mechanism that disconnected teachers from professional accountability and connected them with systems that called for *self-regulation*. The management of teachers' performance is, no more or no less than, the management of teaching.

In an attempt to connect performance management with the professional work of teachers, policy narratives and practices have been increasingly concerned with aligning teachers' work as leaders with the practices of new managerialism. One of the immediate ways in which this was achieved was to ensure that labels such as 'middle leader', 'senior manager' or 'head of department' were attached to tasks such as the allocation, management, auditing and assessment of the work of other teachers.[39] That is, the professional responsibilities of educational leaders have become acutely connected with positional status and in the case of New Zealand, contractually mediated through remuneration and job descriptions that set forth the required (and desired) skills and abilities of the modern leader.

The rhetoric of standards and improvement has been used to pacify public demands, on the one hand[40], and, on the other, to ensure teacher responsiveness to performance management policies and practices that measured their productivity (in terms of student results) and performance. Such systems that emphasise efficiency and accountability accentuate the role of teachers as technicians rather than as professionals that presuppose that teachers cannot be trusted to establish and adhere to their own codes of professional conduct. The underpinning premise is that teachers are primarily motivated by extrinsic rewards and therefore cannot be trusted to serve the common good. Compliance and adherence to managerial demands of the State is therefore secured through performance agreements and performance management that control, regulate and discipline through testing, accountability, standards,

[38]The work of John Smyth and Stephen Ball is instructive here. See John Smyth, 'Teacher Development Against the Policy Reform Grain: An Argument for Recapturing Relationships in Teaching and Learning', *Teacher Development* 11, no. 2 (2007): 221–36; Stephen Ball, 'The Teacher's Soul and the Terror of Performativity', *Journal of Education Policy* 18, no. 2 (2002): 215–28.

[39]Helen M. Gunter and Tanya Fitzgerald, 'Leading Learning and Leading Teachers: Challenges for Schools in the 21st Century', *Leading and Managing* 13, no. 1 (2007): 1–15.

[40]The politics of reform and the apparent public dissatisfaction with the teaching profession has been the subject of intense debate. See, for example, Martin Thrupp, 'Exploring the Politics of Blame: School Inspection and its Contestation in England and New Zealand', *Comparative Education* 34, no. 2 (1998): 195–208. See also John Smyth, 'Undamaging 'Damaged' Teachers: An Antidote to the Self-managing School', *Delta: Policy and Practice in Education* 55, nos. 1–2 (2003): 3–30.

outcomes and quality assurance processes. This continuing lack of trust in teachers, manifested in what Hemmings refers to as a deepening crises of respect,[41] is damaging.[42]

John Smyth has argued that the replacement of leadership that is embedded in pedagogic practices with forms of managerialism is no less than a corruption of leadership.[43] This level of regulation has resulted in the colonisation of teachers' work and professional activities and arguably directed their attention away from pedagogy and pedagogic practices.[44] Education policy and practices that promote the audit and surveillance of teaching are, in my view, misplaced. The attention should be on ways in which productive pedagogy and productive practices occur; not solely on outcomes.[45] Despite almost two decades of educational reform there is little evidence to suggest that school self-management has produced improvements in teaching and learning. Perhaps it is time to suggest that the State cannot be trusted to deliver its objectives.

In much the same way that the number of items that pass through the checkout operator's hands might be counted,[46] marks in examinations as well as other indicators such as increases (or decreases) in literacy and numeracy levels are used to make judgements about a teacher's performance. This is not to suggest that higher education has 'escaped' this panoptic surveillance and disciplinary regimes[47] as exercises such as the Research Assessment Exercise (RAE) in England and the Performance Based Research Fund (PBRF) in New Zealand testify. In addition, discourses such as 'quality assurance', 'reporting', 'inspection', and 'improvement' are co-opted as disciplinary measures to ensure that the 'right' things are being done in the 'right' way. The 'right' way, and I do not use this term accidentally, is, in my view, no less than a mechanism to de-professionalise teachers and teaching so not only are they re-constructed as managed professionals[48] but that schools and students are also managed in particular ways and their 'performance' regulated via OfSTED, ERO, league tables, and public attention. These are the terrors of performativity[49] (what is produced, observed, and measured).[50]

The bureaucratisation of our everyday personal and professional lives and mechanisms of accountability with regards to performance appear to have been unquestionably accepted as the 'right' thing. Invariably too how we might act and react to a variety of circumstances in our professional lives is disciplined insofar as we 'perform' as if we are being watched at every point. It would seem that the threat of failure has effectively created a fear that resistance

---

[41]Annette Hemmings, 'Fighting for Respect in Urban High Schools', *Teachers College Record* 105, no. 3 (2003): 416–37.

[42]The damaging effects of educational policy that is founded on misinformation and marginalised teachers is well argued in John Smyth, 'Policy Research and "Damaged Teachers": Towards an Epistemologically Respectful Paradigm', *Waikato Journal of Education* 10 (2004): 263–81.

[43]John Smyth, 'Unmasking Teachers' Subjectivities in Local School Management', *Journal of Education Policy* 17, no. 4 (2002): 463–82.

[44]See, from example, Pat Mahony and Ian Hextall, *Reconstructing Teaching* (London: RoutledgeFalmer, 2000).

[45]This is more fully explored by Bob Lingard, Debra Hayes, Martin Mills, and Pam Christie, *Leading Learning: Making Hope Practical in Schools* (Maidenhead, UK: Open University Press, 2003).

[46]Charles Fishman, *The Wal-Mart Effect: How an Out-of-Town Superstore Became a Superpower* (London: Allen Lane/Penguin Books, 2006).

[47]Jane Perryman, 'Panoptic Performativity and School Inspection Regimes: Disciplinary Mechanisms and Life under Special Measures', *Journal of Education Policy* 21, no. 2 (2006): 147–61.

[48]Codd, 'Teachers as "Managed Professionals"'.

[49]Ball, 'Teacher's Soul'. This term is attributed to Jean Francois Lyotard, *The Postmodern Condition: A Report on Knowledge*, vol. 10 (Manchester: Manchester University Press, 1984).

[50]Gleeson and Husbands, *Performing School.*

might result in public 'naming and shaming'. If the intention of policy was to create standards by which teachers could be judged, it is misplaced as teachers as professionals are required to submit to policy imperatives that prescribe how they ought to act and react; the technologies of performance which: 'present themselves as techniques of restoring trust (ie accountability, transparency and democratic control) … as such, they presuppose a culture of mistrust in professions and institutions that they themselves contribute to, produce and intensify'.[51]

In other words, policies of performance management are premised on the assumption that teachers cannot be trusted to exercise professional judgement and must therefore be presented with standards and performance measures that script and prescribe what they should and ought to do. Thus, the State and not the profession, determines what 'counts'. This is misplaced policy and it has irrevocably changed the nature of public schooling and teachers work as I have argued at an earlier point.[52]

There can be little doubt that performance management is concerned with ensuring effectiveness in classrooms (judged by measures such as literacy and numeracy tests and examination results) and efficiency at an organisational level (judged by the deployment of resources to meet organisational goals and demands). Effective leaders and effective schools act in particular ways[53] and alongside other regimes such as school inspections, these levels of audit, surveillance and public reporting of performance have become normalised and both accepted and acceptable. This unrelenting focus on performance and standards, rules and regulations has, in complicated ways, interrupted the professional work of teachers. As I argue in the next section, the continuing mistrust of teachers has stimulated the production of a new form of professionalism in which teachers, as 'managed professionals'[54] undertake their work within prescribed boundaries that are positioned as 'commonsense' approaches to teaching and learning.

Managing teachers and teaching

For almost two decades schools in New Zealand and England, although not exclusively or uniformly, have experienced the impact (and threat) of managerialism and modernisation that has served to change the nature of schools (as organisations) and teachers (as professionals). The rhetoric of site-based management was used to seduce teachers, schools and communities that local decision making was both possible and permissible. At one level there were a number of structural changes that occurred to provide schools with a level of administrative responsibility and accountability yet, on the other, increasing surveillance of the work of teachers, schools and their governing bodies through inspection and systems such as performance management, ensured that a level of centralised control remained.[55]

The introduction of regulation and performance management placed increasing emphasis on public accountability of teachers via the creation of a managed profession.[56] As I have

[51]Mitchell Dean, *Governmentality: Power and Rule in Modern Society* (London: Sage, 1999), 169.
[52]See John Smyth, Alistair Dow, Robert Hattam, Alan Reid, and Geoffrey Shacklock, *Teachers' Work in a Globalizing Economy* (London: Falmer, 2000), which outlines the impact of educational reform on teaching and teachers' professional work and identity.
[53]See, for example, the work of Pam Sammons, Josh Hillman, and Peter Mortimore, *Key Characteristics of Effective Schools: A Review of School Effectiveness Research* (London: Institute of Education, 1995). The work of researchers in this area has gained ascendancy in recent times as schools search for eternal solutions in the quest for improved performance by students, teachers and the organisation.
[54]See Codd, 'Teachers as "Managed Professionals"', on this point.
[55]Fitzgerald, 'Remodelling Schools'.
[56]Codd, 'Teachers as "Managed Professionals"'.

outlined, the teaching profession in New Zealand has increasingly been subjected to polices and strategies of surveillance that have served to introduce a culture of managerialism and performativity.[57] Rhetoric suggests that these policies have been underpinned with the desire to create 'a positive framework for improving the quality of teaching and learning'.[58] This is no less than blatant neo-liberal discourse wrapped up in the blanket of 'commonsense' that Apple speaks about;[59] a blanket that masks official policy attempts to define and control what counts as teaching and learning.[60] Not only then are teachers being audited through performance management practices that determine what they should know and be able to do, the adherence to specific curricula and assessment materials further defines what students ought to know and do. Here again I would like to draw attention to two critical questions that Michael Apple continues to ask: Whose knowledge is of most worth? And for what purposes is this official knowledge defined?[61]

These policy changes have produced a new climate in which teachers work; teachers now experience increased hours, increased class sizes, increased administrative tasks, greater accountability and more complex mechanisms for reporting teacher and student outcomes.[62] This has led to a sense of loss of professional autonomy and independent judgement about pedagogy and pedagogic practices. In effect, the State has continued to weaken the education profession through surveillance and control mechanisms that standardise and prescribe what teachers ought to accomplish. Furthermore, the codification of teacher practices as outlined in the *Professional Standards* has introduced a skill hierarchy between teachers (classified as 'beginning', 'classroom' and 'experienced'), 'unit holders' (teachers with additional leadership and management responsibilities and senior leaders (deputy principals and principals).[63] It is highly doubtful as to whether performance management systems, designed to produce more professional and autonomous teachers, will achieve these purposes when, in reality, these are new (seemingly modernised) methods of organisational surveillance, control and conformity.[64] Secondly, although there is no singular definition of what constitutes a 'profession', one of the hallmarks of a profession is the centrality of ownership of knowledge, autonomy and responsibility,[65] as well as a marked absence of hierarchical forms of self-control and the existence of self-regulatory processes. Yet, under regimented policies and practices of performance management, professional autonomy and responsibility is not possible. At the core of these policies and practices is the desire by the State and policy makers to construct a particular set of knowledge, skills, values and attributes for teachers and the profession of teaching. This is the new professionalism that disconnects teachers from pedagogic practices.[66]

---

[57]Jenny Ozga, 'Education: New Labour, New Teachers', in *New Managerialism, New Welfare?*, ed. John Clark, Sharon Gewirtz, and Eugene McLaughlin (London: Sage, 2000).
[58]Ministry of Education, *Professional Standards*, 1.
[59]Apple, *Educating the 'Right' Way.*
[60]This point is also well argued by John Smyth, 'The Politics of Teachers' Work and the Consequences for Schools: Some Implications for Teacher Education', *Asia Pacific Journal of Teacher Education* 34, no. 3 (2006): 301–19.
[61]Apple, *Official Knowledge*, well documents these arguments.
[62]Fitzgerald, 'Remodelling Schools'.
[63]Ministry of Education, *Professional Standards.*
[64]Fitzgerald, 'Remodelling Schools'.
[65]John Furlong, Len Barton, Sheila Miles, and Geoff Whitty, *Teacher Education in Transition* (Buckingham, UK: Open University Press, 2000).
[66]Clarke and Newman suggest that a new managerialism that calls for teachers to be more accountable and efficient and engage in change strategies has emerged. See Clarke and Newman, *The Managerial State.*

The emphasis on hierarchy and regulation has extended to the principalship/headship. Educational reform, while espousing that the principal/head was the professional leader of the school,[67] simultaneously positioned the principal/head as a worker of the managerial State with responsibility and accountability for teacher performance, levels of student achievement, fiscal and strategic management, school improvement initiatives, education policy and legislative compliance as well as overall school performance as determined by the ERO. Accordingly, the principalship has been reformed and additional training and qualifications have assisted with producing the modern leader; a leader that is inevitably gendered, raced and classed.[68] Notwithstanding this point, principalship is subject to intense scrutiny and located as the solution to raising school, teacher and student performance.[69]

Increasingly what is being produced via performance management mechanisms are highly regulated models of what constitutes a 'good' teacher and a 'good' leader; 'good' teachers and leaders who inevitably contribute to the production of 'good' workers and global citizens. As I have outlined in this article, since 1989 the nature of teachers' work and teaching has shifted considerably; from an emphasis on nation building and citizenship[70] to a focus on the knowledge economy and the production of knowledge-based societies. Schooling has therefore mutated from a way of preparing young people for broader purposes (such as participation in a democratic society) to a mechanism of selection and preparation for the local and global labour market. In other words, the *unquestioned* purpose and responsibility of schools is to provide the workforce necessary to compete in the global economy.

To ensure that the needs of the economy and global market place are met, teachers' work has been re-organised 'in such a way as to facilitate the kind of outcome that is required by the State'[71] The curriculum, one of the key areas that was not devolved to local schools in 1989, not only prescribes what teachers ought to do but also determines what 'counts' as official knowledge. In other words, 'good' students will learn 'good' knowledge from 'good' teachers and get 'good' jobs. For this to occur, the agency of teachers has been co-opted to engage in economic and identity work on behalf of the State. The control of teachers' work and ways in which they act (or react) is central to assure the State that 'good' students with 'good' knowledge are being produced. Smyth and his colleagues[72] suggest that there are five particular strategies that contribute to the engineering of compliance and consent from teachers:[73]

(1) *Regulated market control* creates a situation whereby consumers (parents) exercise their economic choices and select a 'good' school for their child; a school that performs to expectations and which has captured market advantage through its own policies and practices. Accordingly, performance management systems as well as public reports from the ERO provide evidence that the school, and its teachers, are meeting their objectives. Not only then is teacher performance subject to scrutiny at an individual level (via his/her line manager), at a school level (via the attestation and registration of teachers), the community can also be assured that teachers and

[67]Government of New Zealand, *Tomorrow's Schools*, 10.
[68]Jill Blackmore, *Troubling Women: Feminism, Leadership and Educational Change* (Buckingham, UK: Open University Press, 1999).
[69]Blackmore and Thomson, '"Good and Bad News"?'.
[70]Apple, *Official Knowledge.*
[71]Smyth et al., *Teachers' Work*, 26.
[72]Smyth et al., *Teachers' Work.*
[73]An earlier version of this analysis appears in Fitzgerald, 'Remodelling Schools'.

their performance are regularly scrutinised. The politics of fear and safety, as alluded to at an earlier point in this article, are therefore played out in numerous ways for the individual, organisation and community.

(2) *Technical control* is exerted through the specification of what is taught (curriculum), how this will be taught (pedagogy) and student outcomes (assessment). In addition, curriculum changes have been from knowledge production to the acquisition of skills; skills that might not necessarily be taught by professionals. In other words, schools are, in the words of the Ministry of Education, future proofed.[74] Or, is it simply the case that schools are teacher proofed? One of the mechanisms to ensure that teachers conform to pre-ordained practices is performance management which serves to reassure the organisation and the State that prescribed routines, policies and practices are being implemented. Performance management is, as I have emphasised in an earlier section, the management of teaching.

(3) *Bureaucratic control* and the bureaucratisation of teaching and teachers' work[75] are imperative to the production of the kinds of outcomes required by the State. Systems such as teacher registration, standards, codes of conduct, attestation and performance management inform the State and its agencies such as the ERO that teachers are performing in expected ways. This level of managerial control and accountability is central to the de-professionalisation of teaching and the determination of what 'counts' and how this counting will occur.

(4) *Corporate control* is a process whereby the governance, management and organisation of schools are derived from the principles and practices of business management as I have outlined at an earlier point. In particular, systems of performance management are the ideal way in which the State can be assured that teachers are both instruments of, instrumental in, and critical to the adoption of neo-liberal reforms.

(5) *Ideological control* is a more subtle process that seeks to advance particular views about what counts as 'good' teaching and being a 'good' teacher. Provided that teachers accept this official knowledge,[76] can produce 'good' students' with 'good' knowledge and collaborate in processes such as performance management which are designed to monitor and judge the standard of their work, then ideological control can be asserted.

What appears missing from policy or any of the documents cited is coherent, robust and independent evidence that evaluates *why* systems of surveillance, regulation and audit of teachers' work and teaching are required. And indeed, despite two decades of monitoring and surveillance of the performance and standards attained by teachers, students, and schools, there is little or no evidence to suggest that anything has 'improved'. In effect, solutions are proposed and implemented in disciplinary ways, when a clearly identified 'problem' does not appear to exist, or at the very least, does not appear to have surfaced. I would like to casually suggest at this point that the introduction of performance and standards is no less than a policy solution and intervention in search of a problem.

[74]Ministry of Education, *Education Priorities for New Zealand* (Wellington: Ministry of Education, 1993).
[75]Fitzgerald, Youngs, and Grootenboer, 'Bureaucratic Control'.
[76]Apple, *Official Knowledge.*

Speaking back

One of the consequences of the economic processes and pressures of the market has been that a great deal of the labour has shifted to the consumer. That is, consumers are now required to be able to assemble furniture items, install computers, scan their own grocery items, make accommodation and travel bookings online, manage their banking electronically, as well as understand advertising and make sense of the information that is packaged with all these 'products'. In a quest to make these products more comprehensible and to assist consumers with their decisions, information is readily available that rates goods, services, and products. In much the same way, ERO reports and league tables of examination results reduce school and teacher performance to 'bite-size' chunks of information for the consumer to collect, collate and utilise in their decision-making processes. Thus, in much the same way as consumers require guarantees and protection from producers and their products, so too can teachers not be trusted unless measurable *public* results are provided and readily available. Consequently, there is the increasing pressure to perform according to imposed and reductive standards that have radically altered the way in which teachers experience their everyday work. Yet (some) teachers are, to an extent, complicit; their own career and professional and advancement depend on the expansion of their expertise as managers (of staff, curricula, and the organisation), their willingness to adopt performance management practices and their ability to demonstrate their responsiveness to schools (product) and parents/students (consumers). Or should a more subtle reading of the current situation be promulgated? That is, teachers act as managers and implement policies such as performance management that originate from the neo-liberal reform agenda precisely because they do not want 'others', presumably those committed to managerial impulses, to be recruited and engaged in these kinds of roles and duties in schools. And as I have commented elsewhere, it is possible that teachers can and do act in professional ways in their performance management practices.[77]

As I have argued to this point, performance management delivered the policy solution to the espoused lack of public confidence. One of the ideological foundations of *Tomorrow's Schools* was that teachers and schools required 'managing' in order for them to become more responsive to the emerging economic climate of the late 1980s. In effect, teachers have been removed from public debate (as have parents, communities and students) and are now required to deliver organisational objectives; objectives that are linked with the demands of the global market place and economic capital. Have teachers become complicit or compliant? Or has performance management re-constructed teachers as obedient and compliant individuals who cannot be trusted to act in professional ways?

There can be little doubt that while, on the one hand, an audit culture such as that which currently exists in schools heightens accountability yet, on the other, this audit culture simultaneously distorts the very nature of what it means to be a professional, belong to a profession, and engage in professional work. The increasing control of the professional work of teachers fosters less, rather than more, trust between professionals and the wider community. But to whom are teachers professionally accountable? In the first phase of reform, the educational reforms were predicated on the call for the public accountability of teachers. Yet, paradoxically, performance management requires teachers to be accountable to the State. How does this then, if at all, restore public confidence and trust in the profession? In what ways, if at all, can accountability enhance rather than diminish trust in the

[77]Fitzgerald, Youngs, and Grootenboer, 'Bureaucratic Control'.

teaching profession? And what is the role of teachers as professionals and academics as professional researchers in speaking back?

The absence of public debate about policies such as performance management underscores my earlier comments about the dangerous times in which we currently live. What appears to be occurring is that 'commonsense' approaches to education policy and policy making are constructed as logical ways to proceed; or at best (or worst), these processes are portrayed as sensible and logical primarily because they are inextricably linked with public demands for accountability. Thus, the creation and maintenance of sustained public debate is seemingly more difficult. Hence, the following can be read as a reasonably prophetic statement:

> The culture in which we live is perhaps the most claustrophobic that has ever existed; in the culture of globalization ... there is no glimpse of an elsewhere, of an otherwise ... The fist step towards building an alternative world has to be a refusal of the world picture implanted in our minds ... Another space is vitally necessary.[78]

In the foreseeable future, I do not envisage that the hegemonic culture and practices of performance management will abate. Indeed, one of the enduring legacies of this new professionalism around what 'counts' as 'good' teaching and learning as I have outlined, is that teachers can determine and calculate their worth. How teachers within an evaluative system may have co-opted these calculative practices is worthy of fuller exploration. As well, the extent to which teachers have used calculative practices to reinterpret their pedagogical practices and choices could also be rich areas of research. I am tendering the suggestion therefore that the policy imperatives such as performance management are not experienced or enacted in universal ways.

Research has been conducted as to ways in which teachers have responded to educational reform.[79] However, these studies could be complemented by fine-grained ethnographic studies that seek to understand the everyday work and professional identities of teachers within an intensified reform agenda; an agenda that increasingly seeks to locate the private sector and its practices as highly desirable.

What I am indicating here is that I fervently believe that teachers are not fully complicit in the de-professionalisation if their work, activities and identities. Recent work conducted by Michael Fielding,[80] John Smyth,[81] as well as Bob Lingard and colleagues,[82] has indicated that teachers can and do speak back to policy narratives. As Helen Gunter and I have argued,[83] the change that has to occur in schools is not just solely structures and hierarchy but that a return to pedagogy and pedagogic relationships are vital. This will therefore require teachers to speak back to policy imperatives and to have the professional courage and conviction to stand up and defend the ethical, moral and pedagogical imperatives on which public (that is, State) schools and schooling were founded.

---

[78]John Berger, *The Shape of a Pocket* (London: Bloomsbury Publishing, 2002), 214.

[79]See from example Smyth, 'Unmasking Teachers' Subjectivities'; Sharon Gewirtz and Stephen Ball, 'From Welfarism to New Managerialism: Shifting Discourses of School Leadership in the Education Marketplace', *Discourse* 21, no. 3 (2000): 253–67.

[80]Michael Fielding, 'Putting the Hands around the Flame: Reclaiming the Radical Tradition of State Education', *Forum* 47, nos. 2–3 (2005): 61–9.

[81]Smyth, 'Teacher Development'.

[82]Lingard et al., *Leading Learning.*

[83]See, for example, Gunter and Fitzgerald, 'Leading Learning'.

Conclusion

There can be little doubt that our everyday personal and professional lives are subject(ed) to control, regulation, monitoring, surveillance and audit activities. The twenty-first century has already been marked with an almost obsessive focus on knowing what individuals do, where and how their activities are conducted and with whom, and imposing sanctions on those who do not conform. As I have pointed out in this paper, there are a number of control forces in play that have *transferred* autonomy and self-regulation from teachers to the State and the global market place. I would argue too the rhetoric of 'self-management' was co-opted to seduce and mislead teachers, schools and communities that they had a real and authentic opportunity to lead and manage their schools. The emphasis on standards and performance of teachers, students and schools, and the increasing powers of agencies such as the ERO and OfSTED would suggest that 'self-management' is a highly centralised system that has led to the bureaucratisation of teachers and teaching.[84] A cynical glance at the New Zealand landscape as portrayed in this article could cause one to wonder if the agenda of the State and its policy makers was to directly makeover schools or takeover the professional work of teachers.[85]

Performance management cannot, by its very nature, produce either a trustworthy profession or stimulate trust in the profession. What is required is a form of professional accountability that rests on the moral and ethical agency of teachers. For this to occur, responsibility and accountability for teachers and their professional work must lie with the profession itself. High trust accountability is both possible and permissible if professional ethics shape and define what constitutes the 'profession' and 'professional' work. This will necessarily involve the teaching profession 'speaking back' and becoming more actively involved in the re-professionalisation of teaching. This therefore requires a reconstruction of teacher professionalism as suggested by Carr and Hartnett:

> …the professionalism of teachers is based on the recognition of their right to make autonomous judgements about how, in particular institutional and classroom contexts, to develop their students' capacity for democratic deliberation, critical judgement and rational understanding. Without this kind of professional autonomy teachers have no protection against external coercion and pressure, and they quickly become neutral operatives implementing the 'directives' of their political masters and mistresses.[86]

I am optimistic that securing high trust and professional accountability is possible if teachers collectively speak back to policies and processes that de-professionalise their work.

---

[84]Fitzgerald, 'Remodelling Schools'.

[85]These terms 'makeover' and 'takeover' draw on the analogy used in reality television that assumes that any intervention results in improved performance or appearance.

[86]Wilfred Carr and Anthony Harnett, *Education and the Struggle for Democracy* (Buckingham, UK: Open University Press, 1996), 195.

School Improvement in a neo-liberal world

Terry Wrigley

Introduction

The concept of 'improvement' is intrinsically ideological. It presents itself as self-evident: *improvement* is obviously a 'good thing', rather like personal hygiene or being kind to animals. Yet improvement also depends upon shared understandings about what kinds of changes are needed. When the aims and direction of change remain tacit, there may be false assumptions about such common understandings. It is only when issues are brought out in open debate that the ideological grip can be broken. A clear-sighted search for improvement depends upon reaching an understanding about the current state of the world, the kind of future we would like to see, and who will benefit from proposed changes. It is salutary to recall that English land enclosures and the Scottish Highland clearances were described in their day as 'improvements', but only by the ruling classes who benefited from them; the evicted peasantry were unconvinced.[1]

The concept of 'improvement' is also problematic because it appears to refer to any measure to make things better. Its actual usages, within the phrase School Improvement, are more situated and more circumscribed, in ways which are rarely acknowledged. It is important, in developing a critical understanding of School Improvement, to raise questions about boundaries and perspectives. For example, in the past year, I have given considerable support,

---

[1]When one looks at landscape paintings of the elegant country houses and estates designed in Jane Austen's time, it is easy to forget who was evicted from the land, and where they went, since they are nowhere to be seen. Similarly, Austen's novels exclude those who laboured to produce the wealth her characters expect and enjoy. Among the many sources for the contrasting class-based understandings of enclosures and clearances, see Jane Humphries 'Enclosures, Common Rights, and Women: The Proletarianisation of Families in the Late Eighteenth and Early Nineteenth Centuries', *Journal of Economic History* 50, no. 1 (1990): 17–42. See also James Symonds, 'Toiling in the Vale of Tears: Everyday Life and Resistance in South Uist, Outer Hebrides, 1760–1860', *International Journal of Historical Archaeology* 3, no. 2 (1999): 101–22.

as an engaged academic, to the Anti-Academies Alliance.[2] I was also involved in a successful campaign to stop school closures in my own city of Edinburgh in September 2007.[3] Both these campaigns were about protecting and improving educational provision, yet it would be difficult to have them classified as School Improvement work. This cannot be an issue of pure versus applied research, since most established School Improvement experts also operate as consultants, often combining these two roles. The issue is more probably a tacit one of political alignment.[4]

A coherent and honest School Improvement theory can only be built upon declared ethical and political positions. To shelter behind technical or managerial neutrality ('what works') is inherently conservative, as it falsely assumes the truth value of the status quo and reinforces hegemonic frames of reference. It is widely understood that School Effectiveness is characterised by such technicism; similarly, on a practical level, the accountability regime which Nikolas Rose has called 'government by number'.[5] It is not so widely accepted that School Improvement, in its dominant version, suffers from a parallel limitation. Because it overlooks pedagogical and sociological ideas and claims to provide a universally applicable approach to change management, it reduces Improvement to a value- and context-free technical issue. This is often difficult to recognise because School Improvement maintains a utopian aura through its continued use of keywords such as vision, mission and values; and because of its insistence that establishing consensus among participants is required in order to effect sustainable change. One of the arguments in this paper will be that a transformation took place in England, in the early 1990s, of a paradigm which was fundamentally progressive and democratic into one which still wore the clothes – a neat ideological shift.

The argument in this paper is necessarily only an outline. Firstly, there is space only for limited substantiation through some key examples. Secondly, it is built almost entirely round the context of the English education system. Thirdly, the attempt to describe a paradigm may fail to take into account the centrifugal forces, including individuals who have partly at least broken away and are pursuing other interests. Despite these reservations, I believe that the paradigm has been disseminated and accepted in many other contexts, thanks in part to agencies such as the OECD and the World Bank; it will be interesting to receive comments from readers working in other contexts as to its wider validity as an analysis. Moreover, even if, in its English heartland, every single one of its original adherents had abandoned ship, the paradigm argument would still hold true since it has been fully institutionalised.

---

[2]The Academies are schools which are publicly funded but privately managed. This neo-liberal privatisation is being pursued by England's New Labour government, despite evidence that it is not benefiting the urban populations it was supposed to serve (see www.antiacademies.org.uk).

[3]The Education Authority sought to justify its closures by a claim that 'research shows' larger schools to be more effective. It was important to correct this summary.

[4]A further example of this has been the resounding silence of the English School Improvement experts when prime minister Blair embarked on a discourse of derision concerning 'bog-standard comprehensive schools'. See Clyde Chitty and Brian Simon, eds., *Promoting Comprehensive Education in the 21st Century* (Stoke-on-Trent, UK: Trentham Books, 2001). The end of selection at age 11 removed a major obstacle to raising educational standards and qualifications, but is scarcely mentioned in the literature as a 'school improvement'. See Sally Tomlinson, 'Selection, Diversity and Inequality', *Improving Schools* 5, no. 3 (2003): 6–12; Jürgen Baumert and Gundel Schümer, 'Family Background, Selection and Achievement: The German Experience', *Improving Schools* 5, no. 3 (2003): 13–20.

[5]Nikolas Rose, *Powers of Freedom: Reframing Political Thought* (Cambridge: Cambridge University Press, 1999).

Understanding paradigms

The Kuhnian concept of paradigm has sometimes been associated with relativism.[6] Though Kuhn does sometimes lay himself open to this interpretation[7], thinking about paradigms can also be liberating, in that it historicises and denaturalises hegemonic models and ideologies. It gives us a tool to grasp the inner logic of a dominant way of thinking and acting; to perceive links between knowledge and power (Foucault[8]); and to open up spaces of possibility within an apparently stable or closed system.

Although Kuhn recognises the operation of subjective and inter-subjective factors in scientific change, paradigms should not be seen as a question of academic fashions. His work emphasises the deep-rooted nature of paradigms, involving ontological and epistemological as well as methodological shifts. He first applied the word *paradigms* to exemplary discoveries, experiments and texts which set a standard for a school of scientific thought.[9] He then extended the term from the trigger to the result, to 'all the shared commitments of a scientific group' including its 'instrumental, theoretical and metaphysical commitments'.[10] One can summarise his concept of paradigms as involving:

- entities, forces and laws – key concepts, relationships and causes;
- models – whether seen as heuristic or ontological;
- legitimate problems and acceptable solutions;
- methods and instruments.

Extending the term into the realm of social sciences presented a number of challenges.[11] Though the issue was sometimes discussed in terms of a methodological conflict – quantitative versus qualitative, the 'paradigms wars' of the 1980s – more thorough discussions[12] explored and clarified the links between methodology, epistemology and ontological assumptions; the ethical and political dimensions of paradigm disagreements; and the consequences when research paradigms become institutionalised within a policy regime. For example, in the field of education, Eisner argues that positivistic modes of evaluation have a deep impact upon teaching and learning:

---

[6]See, for example, Christopher Norris, *Against Relativism: Philosophy of Science, Deconstruction and Critical Theory* (Oxford: Blackwell, 1997), 82–96. Norris regards Kuhn as a contributor to the growth of relativism which blossomed in the post-modernist movement.

[7]This is partly through his use of the term 'incommensurable', derived from the committed relativist Feyerabend. Kuhn also causes confusion by sliding between 'world' and 'world-view' in some texts. For an extended discussion, see Paul Hoyningen-Huene, *Reconstructing Scientific Revolutions: Thomas S Kuhn's Philosophy of Science* (London: University of Chicago Press, 1993). A realist interpretation would argue that paradigm shifts are triggered because of the contradictions between the material world and cognitive models, and through the persistent intrusions of material reality upon scientists' world-views.

[8]This theme characterises much of Michel Foucault's work, but a useful introduction is *Power/Knowledge: Selected Interviews and Other Writings 1972–1984* (London: Routledge, 1990).

[9]Originally paradigm was a grammatical term. It designated a single example used to illustrate a declension of nouns or a conjugation of verbs.

[10]Thomas Samuel Kuhn, *The Structure of Scientific Revolutions*, 2nd ed. (Chicago: University of Chicago Press, 1970), 297.

[11]Originally Kuhn had argued that the social sciences had no paradigms or were 'pre-paradigmatic', by which he meant that no school of thought had unquestioned dominance. He later conceded that in such a situation each school had its own paradigms, in the sense of influential exemplars. See Kuhn, *Structure of Scientific Revolutions*, Postscript, 178–9, note 10.

[12]See principally the conference proceedings represented in Egon G. Guba, ed., *The Paradigm Dialog* (London: Sage, 1990).

> What we count counts. What we measure matters. What we test, we teach. After all, adaptation is a primary form of survival, and our appetite for assessment requires forms of adaptation in teaching that makes survival possible … Policy that publishes in local newspapers the achievement test scores of students on standardised tests on a school-by-grade basis reveals a set of values about what really counts in that school district and inevitably influences what teachers are likely to attend to in their classrooms.[13]

An interesting illustration from a field of social practice of the need for a multi-level understanding of paradigms can be found in the psychiatric work of R.D. Laing. Commenting on Goffman's *Asylums*,[14] Laing shows the interconnection of ontological assumptions, epistemological judgements, methodological procedures, ethical consequences and institutional norms:

> A large part of his study [i.e. Goffman's *Asylums*] is devoted to a detailed documentation of how it comes about that a person, in being put in the role of patient, tends to become defined as a non-agent, as a non-responsible object, to be treated accordingly, and even comes to regard himself in this light.[15]

He argues for a social-phenomenological rather than clinical approach to diagnosis, in order to focus on the complex way in which human beings make sense of each other and of social situations and events.[16] Later in this article I will attempt to draw upon Laing's critique of traditional psychiatric practice in proposing alternatives to the hegemonic School Improvement paradigm.

To summarise provisionally, my argument is that a sufficient understanding of paradigms in the humanities and social sciences, as also within fields of social practice such as education, requires consideration of multiple levels:

- entities and the forces/relationships that connect them;
- models and theories;
- legitimate problems and acceptable solutions;
- methods and instruments;
- political frames;
- ethical considerations.

By *political*, I mean primarily that a paradigm might privilege some perspectives and interests more than others, or it might overlook important differences of power. By *ethical*, I am referring both to the researcher's and the practitioner's (e.g. administrator's or manager's) responsibility for moral evaluation of practice, as opposed to more technicist judgements about 'what works'.

These latter dimensions will facilitate a critique of hegemonic School Improvement, and its operation within a wider neo-liberal world and world-view. To ignore them is to reinforce ideology, by allowing the operations of power to remain invisible: 'Power is at its most effective when least observable'.[17] '[Power] is tolerable only on condition that it

---

[13] Elliott W. Eisner, 'The Meaning of Alternative Paradigms for Practice', in *The Paradigm Dialog*, ed. Egon G. Guba (London: Sage, 1990), 94–6.
[14] Erving Goffman, *Asylums: Essays on the Social Situation of Mental Patients and Other Inmates* (Garden City, NY: Doubleday, 1961).
[15] Ronald David Laing, *The Politics of Experience* (Harmondsworth, UK: Penguin, 1967), 92.
[16] Ibid., 15.
[17] Steven Lukes, *Power: A Radical View*, 2nd ed. (Basingstoke, UK: Palgrave Macmillan, 2005), 1.

mask a substantial part of itself. Its success is proportional to its ability to hide its own mechanisms'.[18]

These various layers cannot be separated from one another. The political and ethical interconnect with the ontological and epistemological.[19]

School Improvement: a paradigm shift[20]

The origins of School Improvement as a theory and set of guidelines for educational change are frequently described in terms of an implementation-failure of centrally mandated innovation.[21] This narrative of origins is, in the English context at least, somewhat exaggerated. Unlike the USA, where deliberate attempts were made to design 'teacher-proof' curricular packages, the various School Council projects of the 1970s and thereabouts gave careful thought to teacher engagement in the design and implementation processes.[22] Even so, clear gains were made in terms of a developing understanding of change processes. The need to recognise teacher agency in innovation, as well as the backward pull of professional habits, led to a greater emphasis in the literature concerning change processes on deep discussion and understanding of aims as well as methods.

Until the 1990s, there was remarkably little connection[23] between School Improvement (qualitative) and School Effectiveness (quantitative), despite some important mixed-method studies.[24] The statistical School Effectiveness analyses which sought to identify

---

[18]Michel Foucault, *Power/Knowledge: Selected Interviews and Other Writings 1972–77* (Brighton, UK: Harvester, 1980), 86.

[19]Similarly, Gronn makes the point that leadership became a favoured entity in education, privileged over, and disconnected from, a family of similar terms which designate 'modes of human conduct and engagement' such as 'power, authority, influence, manipulation, force and persuasion'. This is a pertinent illustration of how methodology depends upon discourses, which themselves contain ontological as well as political assumptions, operating as much through their silences and closures as by what they speak. Peter Gronn, 'Distributing and Intensifying School Leadership', in *Rethinking Educational Leadership: Challenging the Conventions*, ed. Nigel Bennett and Lesley Anderson (London: Sage, 2003), 60.

[20]Some of the tensions and issues discussed in this section echo those in William Foster, *Paradigms and Promises: New Approaches to Educational Administration* (Amherst, NY: Prometheus Books, 1986). Foster opposes the dominant technical rationalism of the field in the USA and argues that educational administration should be constructed as a 'moral science'.

[21]See, for example, Milbrey McLaughlin, 'The Rand Change Agent Study Revisited: Macro Perspectives, Micro Realities', *Educational Researcher* 19, no. 9 (1990): 11–16.

[22]Substantial evidence can be found in Lawrence Stenhouse, *Authority, Education and Emancipation* (London: Heinemann, 1983) and Lawrence Stenhouse, ed., *Curriculum Research and Development in Action* (London: Heinemann, 1980).

[23]This is acknowledged by such key figures as Reynolds and Fullan, representing both sides of the Effectiveness/Improvement divide. Michael Fullan, *The New Meaning of Educational Change* (London: Cassell, 1991), 5 seq; Michael Fullan, *Successful School Improvement* (Buckingham, UK: Open University Press, 1992), 21 seq; David Reynolds and Charles Teddlie, with David Hopkins and Sam Stringfield, 'Linking School Effectiveness and School Improvement', in *The International Handbook of School Effectiveness Research*, ed. David Reynolds and Charles Teddlie (London: RoutledgeFalmer, 2000), 207–8.

[24]A key example is a study of urban primary schools commissioned by the Inner London Education Authority. Peter Mortimore, Pamela Sammons, Louise Stoll, David Lewis, and Russell Ecob, *School Matters: The Junior Years* (Wells, UK: Open Books, 1988).

'key characteristics' of more successful schools resulted in lists which were often difficult to operationalise.[25] There were several reasons for this:

(1) the characteristics described were often unclear: what, for example, is 'strong' leadership, or 'a focus on teaching and learning'?[26]
(2) lines and directions of causality were not well identified, assumptions being made that the key characteristics which correlated with certain outcomes were the direct causes of these outcomes;
(3) the interaction of these various characteristics was not well understood, despite a realisation by Rutter et al.[27] that the combined and cumulative effect was greater than the sum of the parts;
(4) these various factors were assumed to have a similar enhancing effect in all situations, though they might prove more difficult to implement in areas of greater poverty or ethnic diversity.

The first point is particularly important in understanding the workings of School Effectiveness in policy and practice. These floating signifiers are not simply too vague to be operational; they are too easily appropriated, with a particular accent, into the dominant discourses and practices which approve of certain types of leadership and teaching.

The need for a more holistic view and intervention was clearly understood by School Improvement researchers, including transformations across a school.[28] Learning from systematic initiatives such as the Halton[29] district of Ontario, an emphasis was placed upon building the school's *capacity* for change as well as implementing specific changes. Despite radically different methodologies, and clear reservations about the other's methods, marriage proposals were discussed and promoted between School Effectiveness and School Improvement. Significant steps in this process included establishing ICSEI (the International Congress of School Effectiveness and Improvement) in 1988, and founding its journal *School Effectiveness and School Improvement* two years later.[30]

The tensions in this move can be understood by reading Hopkins, the leading English School Improvement writer, who describes the advantages of Improvement over Effectiveness:

- a 'bottom-up' orientation – improvement is owned by the individual school and its staff;
- qualitative research methodology;

[25]See, for example, discussion in Roland Barth, *Improving Schools from Within* (San Francisco: Jossey-Bass, 1990).
[26]It may be easier to identify 'weak leadership' than to clarify what one means by 'strong'; similarly, a lack of focus on teaching and learning is easier to agree upon than the value of a particular pedagogical orientation.
[27]Michael Rutter, Janet Ouston, Peter Mortimore and Barbara Maugham, *Fifteen Thousands Hours* (London: Open Books, 1979), 177–9.
[28]In part, this relates to an international trend towards greater autonomy for schools, although in England local management of schools was accompanied by much tighter central control of the curriculum and a quasi-market built largely upon competitive advantage in national tests.
[29]This formed the practical foundation for the work of Michael Fullan and colleagues at OISE, University of Toronto, and was transported to England by Louise Stoll.
[30]Whereas the Journal has tended towards effectiveness studies, the Congress has often opened up to other voices in educational change, depending partly on where it has taken place and that year's planning team.

- concern with changing organisational processes rather than the outcomes of the school;
- concern to treat educational outcomes as not 'given' but problematic;
- a concern to see schools as dynamic institutions requiring extended study more than 'snapshop' cross-sectional studies.[31]

It is clear which approach Hopkins favours. Despite this, he was a leading proponent of deliberately linking together Improvement and Effectiveness. A key document on this process is 'Linking School Effectiveness Knowledge and School Improvement Practice: Towards a Synergy',[32] written with Louise Stoll (a member of Mortimore's Schools Matter team) and David Reynolds (arguably the leading British School Effectiveness expert). The authors speak openly of paradigms and paradigmatic change, but view these primarily as methodological issues, to the neglect of ontological, epistemological and ethical dimensions. They are silent about the political context they are working in, and their marriage proposal begs many of the questions that my own and others' work has had to grapple with.

This planned merger and paradigm change, the creation of an Effectiveness-linked School Improvement paradigm, had a number of consequences:

(1) Given the policy environment, there has been a tendency to understand ostensibly open-ended references to 'educational outcomes' predominantly in terms of test and exam results. This is inevitable, in the absence of any comment to the contrary, and because the new paradigm eschews philosophical debates about educational aims.
(2) The avoidance of philosophical and pedagogical discussion renders the new paradigm managerialist, in the sense that change management is all. Curriculum is something decided by government, and teaching is reduced to the efficient transmission of that curriculum, i.e. its 'delivery'.
(3) There is a parallel neglect of sociology, alongside a diminished sense of community and context. Both the internal ethos of the school and the role of parents and the wider community are viewed instrumentally, as a vehicle towards the raising of test scores. To parody Bourdieu, the world has become weightless.[33]
(4) A failure to challenge the policy context leads quickly to a betrayal of the democratic potential which characterised School Improvement. The role of school management becomes one of persuading teachers to want exactly what government decides they must want.[34]

---

[31]David Hopkins, *School Improvement for Real* (London: RoutledgeFalmer, 2001), 56.
[32]David Reynolds, David Hopkins, and Louise Stoll, 'Linking School Effectiveness Knowledge and School Improvement Practice: Towards a Synergy', *School Effectiveness and School Improvement* 4, no. 1 (1993): 37–58.
[33]Angus' comments on School Effectiveness apply almost as much to the dominant version of School Improvement: 'Family background, social class, any notion of context are typically regarded as "noise", as "outside background factors" which must be controlled for and then stripped away so that the researcher can concentrate on the important domain of school factors'. Lawrence Angus, 'The Sociology of School Effectiveness', *British Journal of Sociology of Education* 14, no. 3 (1993): 361. The Bourdieu allusion is to *The Weight of the World* (Stanford, CA: Stanford University Press, 1999).
[34]'The problems of the education system have been laid at the door of teachers while their capacity for finding solutions has been taken away. The rhetoric has been of empowerment, participation and teams, but the reality is that teachers have had to continue to do what they have always done – be empowered to do what they have been told to do.' Helen Gunter, *Leaders and Leadership in Education* (London: Chapman, 2001), 144.

It is arguable that this new version of School Improvement amounts to little more than *soft management of hard policy*.

There are inevitably differences in the extent to which those identifying as part of the School Improvement camp fit this description, even in the English context, and it is beyond the scope of this paper to examine the extent of its influence internationally.[35] Within the English education system, Michael Barber perhaps epitomises this development, and was certainly very active in re-orienting others towards the 'Standards'[36] agenda which dominates both Thatcherite and Blairite policy. Barber rose meteorically from being a teacher's union official via two very brief professorships to heading up school improvement at the Department for Education. Whilst continuing to wear the School Improvement colours, he effectively negated its emphasis on collegial participation by centrally mandating[37] exactly how teachers would structure and teach their lessons. This went beyond the National Curriculum introduced by Thatcher as Prime Minister, in two key respects:

(1) curriculum content had been determined within a two- to four-year timespan (the Key Stages) but was now dictated term by term, at least throughout primary schools;
(2) the centralised control now extended beyond curriculum content and summative assessment to the minutiae of teaching.

Barber was later to justify this by citing the thoughts of Pascal: 'To show the peasants how to pray, first you must get them on their knees'.[38]

Some of the key figures in School Improvement remained uncomfortable with such policy shifts, but failed to oppose them publicly. A recurrent trope was to voice some criticism in the opening chapter of a book before continuing to counsel headteachers towards a participatory approach as if nothing had been said or the problems did not matter. It was almost as if teachers should simply take on trust the wisdom of government policy decisions and commit themselves wholeheartedly to furthering them; the result was 'contrived collegiality'.[39] Thrupp and Willmott have fittingly described this compromised position as 'subtle apologism'.[40]

It is debatable whether this attempt to marry School Effectiveness and School Improvement actually succeeded. There have been enduring tensions between 'mechanistic' and 'organic' accounts of school development.[41] Chapman argues that programmes located within the effectiveness tradition tend to be more mechanistic, whilst those located within

[35]My own position is that, despite the global spread, there are significant variations. In Spain, for example, school improvement is largely about school-initiated curriculum development projects. See, for example, the various case studies in F. Javier Murillo and Mercedes Muñoz-Repiso, eds., *La Mejora de la Escuela: Un Cambio de Mirada* (Barcelona: Octaedro, 2002).

[36]The term Standards is used here as a shorthand for a policy regime focused explicitly and overwhelmingly on raising test scores.

[37]I use this word to recall McLaughlin's influential sentence disseminated internationally by Michael Fullan, 'Policy cannot mandate what matters'. McLaughlin, 'Rand Change Agent Study', 12.

[38]This is taken from a report on Barber's contribution to a conference on Education Action Zones. Ken Jones, 'Responding to the Themes of the Collection', in Chitty and Simon, *Promoting Comprehensive Education*, 88.

[39]Andy Hargreaves, *Changing Teachers, Changing Times* (London: Cassell, 1994).

[40]Martin Thrupp and Robert Willmott, *Educational Management in Managerialist Times: Beyond the Textual Apologists* (Maidenhead, UK: Open University Press, 2003).

[41]Alma Harris, 'What Works in School Improvement? Lessons from the Field and Future Directions', *Educational Research* 42, no. 1 (2000): 1–11.

Table 1. Summary of principal characteristics of School Effectiveness-linked School Improvement.

Entities, forces, laws (ontological)	A focus on the school as a manageable unit, in which change is brought about through leadership and internal collaboration.
Models and theories	A model of change which focuses on transforming attitudes and habits particularly among teachers, with a tendency to neglect pedagogical or sociological explanations.
Legitimate problems and acceptable solutions	An overwhelming orientation to the key problem of improving test results, supported by practices which 'raise capacity' for sustainable improvement into the future.
Methods and instruments	An emphasis on processes of persuasion and collaboration, whole-school planning, networking, providing vision, staff development, whilst also incorporating accountability data as a motivator/threat.
Political frames	A compliance with external regulations (the accountability regime, curriculum, particular teaching methods) and a pragmatic failure to raise questions of power and social injustice.
Ethical considerations	A general subordination of social and moral values to quantifiable success indicators.

the improvement tradition tend to be more organic in nature.[42] It is more appropriate, I believe, to speak of a new Improvement paradigm which, despite some counter currents, has largely reorientated itself to the aims and perspectives of School Effectiveness, and has adapted to a neo-liberal political environment. Table 1 attempts to summarise the dominant (though not uncontested) features of this new version of Improvement, using the framework offered in the preceding section.

Culture

The term 'culture' became a keyword signifying a shift to a more holistic and less mechanistic perspective. Rutter et al., in their classic *Fifteen Thousand Hours*,[43] had concluded that the *combined and cumulative* effect of various factors was more important than any individual effectiveness characteristics. It is ironic that, in adopting the term culture – according to Raymond Williams,[44] 'one of the two or three most complicated words in the English language' – School Improvement writers missed a great opportunity to deepen their thinking.

Culture had already been deployed in diverse and rich ways in educational research, including ethnographic studies (Willis, McLaren etc.) which relate schooling to the wider society, and their intersection in the lives of young people, especially in working-class neighbourhoods;[45] and a large body of texts relating class, culture and curriculum by writers such as James Britton, Harold Rosen, Nell Keddie, Eric Midwinter, Harold Entwistle, Denys Lawton and others. Bourdieu and Passeron used the term 'cultural capital' to enable us to reflect on ways in which schools succeed or fail to value family and neighbourhood

[42]Christopher Chapman, *Improving Schools through External Intervention* (London: Continuum, 2005), 17.
[43]Rutter et al., *Fifteen Thousands Hours*.
[44]Raymond Williams, *Keywords: A Vocabulary of Culture and Society* (London: Fontana, 1976), 87.
[45]Paul Willis, *Learning to Labour: How Working Class Kids Get Working Class Jobs* (Farnborough, UK: Saxon House, 1977); Peter McLaren, *Schooling as a Ritual Performance: Towards a Political Economy of Education Symbols and Gestures* (London: RKP, 1987).

culture.[46] Sarason had deployed the term to have us think about the tacit norms of schooling; he is frequently cited by Stoll and others but his original intention has been lost.[47]

Unfortunately School Improvement has tended to adopt a set of meanings derived mainly from business management – the need to 'manage the culture' of a corporation or site. Culture equates with cohesion or even manageability.[48]

Louise Stoll[49] provides an exemplary summary of culture as deployed in orthodox School Improvement texts, but one which unconsciously exposes its own limitations. Despite briefly acknowledging (on pages 33 and 35) an anthropological sense of culture as significant 'customs, rituals, symbols, stories and language – the artefacts of culture', Stoll largely follows Schein[50] in stripping away the materiality in favour of a 'deeper level of basic assumptions and beliefs that are shared by members of an organisation'. These words are revealing: in which sense are different people 'members', and how exactly are these assumptions and beliefs 'shared'? Who, for that matter, decides what is 'basic'? A list is provided of 'Norms of Improving Schools'[51] which expresses culture in terms of positive feelings among staff:

(1) Shared goals – 'we know where we're going'.
(2) Responsibility for success – 'we must succeed'.
(3) Collegiality – 'we're working on this together', etc.

There is some value in this summary, but as the *Weltanschauung* of School Improvement, it is bland and one-dimensional, taking little account of the many contradictions, of teachers' and pupils' lives outside, and of external pressures both political and socioeconomic. There is no concession that some innovations might be ill-conceived, that professionals have a right and duty to evaluate them critically, or that some changes should be resisted. There is a warm glow about this notion of culture, emphasising a rather uncritical cohesion, which can conceal some of the turmoil outside.

Cultural leadership for School Improvement requires a more political and contextualised exploration of culture, and specifically in relation to demands for greater democracy and to the achievement of success in inner-city schools. For example:

- exploring the differences between authoritarian and co-operative cultures, including developing new rituals for co-operative and democratic learning;
- examining the cultural significance of alienated forms of learning, in which, like factory work, you are told what to write and then hand over your product not to an

[46] Pierre Bourdieu and Jean-Claude Passeron, *Reproduction in Education, Society and Culture* (1970; repr., London: Sage, 1977).

[47] Seymour Sarason, *The Culture of the School and the Problem of Change* (Boston: Allyn and Bacon, 1971).

[48] A sharp critique of this reductionist use of the term can be found in Mats Alvesson, *Understanding Organizational Culture* (London: Sage, 2002). We owe the argument that the central role of leadership is to 'manage culture' to Terrence E. Deal and Kent D. Peterson, *Shaping School Culture* (San Francisco: Jossey-Bass, 1999). Again, there has been a tendency towards selective summary and citation, since this work also includes a call to recognise the complex and creative cultural work of school leaders, including the roles of 'historian, anthropological sleuth, visionary, symbolist, potter, poet, actor and healer' (87–8).

[49] Louise Stoll, 'School Culture: Black Hole or Fertile Garden for School Improvement', in *School Culture*, ed. Jon Prosser (London: Chapman, 1999).

[50] Edgar Schein, *Organisational Culture and Leadership* (San Francisco: Jossey-Bass, 1985).

[51] Stoll, 'School Culture', 37. The list originally appeared in Louise Stoll and Dean Fink, Changing our Schools: Linking School Effectiveness and School improvement (Buckingham: Open University Press, 1996).

interested audience but to the teacher-as-examiner, for token payment in the form of a mark or grade;

- questioning the culture of target setting and surveillance which regulates the lives of pupils and teachers, and exploring more democratic forms of educational responsibility than the present accountability culture;
- examining the cultural messages of classrooms which are dominated by the teacher's voice, closed questions and rituals of transmission of superior wisdom;
- developing a better understanding of cultural difference, in order to prevent high levels of exclusion;
- understanding how tacit assumptions about 'ability' and 'intelligence' are worked out in classroom interactions;
- discovering how tacit assumptions about single parents and 'dysfunctional' working-class families operate symbolically in classroom interactions.[52]

It should be noted that these issues stretch way beyond teacher attitudes towards change, and connect sociological and pedagogical perspectives.

Similarly, Richard Bates has argued for a return to richer anthropological uses of *culture.* He emphasises the need to recognise the multiple realities in a state of tension within any organisation, the production of meaning through struggle and their articulation through language, symbols and performance. He insists on the incompatibility between a rich sense of culture as meaning-giving and the perspective of managerial manipulation. He seeks to refocus our attention on ways in which the 'cultural battles of the wider society' are 'carried into the school by individuals and groups'.[53] He looks in great detail at the many ways in which material objectives and actions have symbolic effect in schools in a groundbreaking paper 'Aesthetics, Educational Leadership and Management'.[54]

Poverty

I have argued above that the dominant School Improvement paradigm regards curriculum as a given, reduces pedagogical questions to efficient transmission, and treats school ethos and wider community relations instrumentally. There is a prima facie case for questioning such a paradigm in contexts of poverty and disadvantage. It takes little insight to propose the following hypotheses:

- that a centrally prescribed and standardised curriculum might need greater adaptation in order to engage working-class or ethnic minority pupils in meaningful learning;
- that a deeper and better theorised pedagogical enquiry is needed to help under-achieving pupils;
- that relationships with parents and the local community are potentially more problematic and require more effort and thought, where there is a greater social and cultural gap between teachers and parents, where the community is in any way troubled, or if parents have reasons to be disillusioned with or antipathetic towards schools.

---

[52]The list is drawn from Terry Wrigley, *Schools of Hope: A New Agenda for School Improvement* (Stoke-on-Trent, UK: Trentham: 2003), 36–7.

[53]Richard Bates, 'Culture and Leadership in Educational Administration: An Historical Study of What Was and What Might Have Been', *Journal of Educational Administration and History* 38, no. 2 (2006): 155–68.

[54]Richard Bates, 'Aesthetics, Educational Leadership and Management', in *International Encyclopaedia of Education*, 3rd ed. (Dordrecht: Springer, 2008).

Despite this, and despite recent concerns about what government officials in England euphemistically call 'schools in challenging circumstances', there has been considerable neglect in the Effectiveness and the Improvement literature of schools serving high-poverty neighbourhoods.[55] This is all the more surprising given the narrative of origin of School Effectiveness, in which it claims the moral high-ground for rejecting reproduction theories as negative and fatalistic.

Whilst arguing against the narrow attainment focus of the current Improvement paradigm, it is nevertheless important to state that formal qualifications are of high importance for working-class and ethnic minority pupils. Indeed, if you have the 'wrong' postcode or skin colour, you need such qualifications more than anyone. In a hierarchical society, education is a positional good as well as a good in itself and a good for the world. The problem is that an overemphasis on test and exam results can become counterproductive:

(1) insufficient attention is paid to the recognition (identity, self-esteem) aspect of social justice[56] which underpins personal struggles to succeed in school and in later life;
(2) an overwhelming emphasis on the exchange value of learning can result in curriculum and pedagogy which lack enjoyment and engagement.[57]

It should be emphasised that a strong link between socio-economic[58] background and attainment is an international problem, albeit to varying degrees. The PISA (Programme for International Student Assessment) data of almost all countries shows that students in the lowest socio-economic quarter are between two and three times as likely to be in the lowest attaining quarter in language, mathematics and science.[59] The prominent role of School Improvement in the English education system has done little to reduce the link between poverty and low achievement.[60]

The case against School Effectiveness has been well rehearsed.[61] There is, for example, scarcely a mention of poverty in the encyclopaedic *International Handbook*.[62] In the UK at

---

[55]This judgement is confirmed by Christopher Chapman, *Improving Schools through External Intervention* (London: Continuum, 2005), 20, which also lists the chief exceptions. Similarly by Alma Harris and Jane McGregor in their introduction to Paul Clarke, ed., *Improving Schools in Difficulty* (London: Continuum, 2005).

[56]Nancy Fraser, *Justice Interruptus: Critical Reflections on the 'Postsocialist' Condition* (London: Routledge, 1997).

[57]See, for example, the very powerful argument on literacy and identity in Jim Cummins, 'Challenging the Construction of Difference as Deficit: Where Are Identity, Intellect, Imagination, and Power in the New Regime of Truth?', in *Pedagogies of Difference: Rethinking Education for Social Change*, ed. Peter Pericles Trifonas (London: RoutledgeFalmer, 2003).

[58]To be exact, we should add the word 'cultural' to social and economic, given the importance of factors such as parental education which is not always matched to the household's current economic situation, particularly in the case of well-educated single mothers.

[59]These data are reproduced as tables 2.1.1, 2.2.1 and 2.3.1 of the OECD review of the quality and equity of education outcomes in Scotland: diagnostic report, www.oecd.org/edu/reviews/nationalpolicies.

[60]In his 2003 Annual Report the Chief Inspector noted 'that the gap between the average achievement in the highest performing schools and the lowest continues to widen'. Office for Standards in Education (2003, para. 79). More detailed research on attainment differentials related to socioeconomic background is to be found in Robert Cassen and Geeta Kingdon, *Tackling Low Educational Achievement* (York, UK: Joseph Rowntree Foundation, 2007).

[61]See Terry Wrigley, 'School Effectiveness: The Problem of Reductionism', *British Educational Research Journal* 30, no. 2 (2004): 227–44.

[62]Charles Teddlie and David Reynolds, *International Handbook of School Effectiveness Research* (London: RoutledgeFalmer, 2000).

least, the mainstream School Improvement literature, despite having recourse to the same justification and narrative of origin, produced few texts focusing on social class or poverty from around the mid-1990s, though this began to change around 2005 due to an increased concern by the government department. The important exceptions have been *Success Against the Odds* in 1996[63] along with its 2001 successor volume;[64] Stoll and Myers' *No Quick Fixes*[65] in 1998; and four recent volumes connected to Department for Education and Skills commissions and projects, Clarke (2005), Harris et al. (2006), Ainscow and West (2006) and Macbeath et al. (2007).[66] Among these, two books do not follow the usual patterns: Clarke's book includes a commissioned chapter from myself and also Richard Riddell, whilst Macbeath et al. rigorously challenge the conclusions reached by Harris et al. I will comment briefly on Stoll and Myers's *No Quick Fixes* as an illustration, partly because it represents almost a pantheon of English School Improvement and School Effectiveness experts: in addition to its editors, there are chapters by Barber, Hopkins, Harris, MacBeath, Learmonth, Lodge, Reynolds as well as North Americans Fink (School Improvement) and Stringfield (School Effectiveness), and various lesser known authors. It was also written as these paradigms were actively 'twinning', and as the New Labour project was becoming a reality.

In this book, there is a stunning silence about the poverty in which so many children grow up; rather these children are viewed from the school's perspective as a kind of obstacle. Returning to my paradigm points, the school is the key entity and field, with the dominant characteristics and narratives of children's lives viewed as mere background difficulties. Ethnicity is scarcely mentioned, except on two occasions where minorities are themselves blamed for creating difficulties.[67]

The solutions proposed throughout this volume are almost all managerial in nature, focusing around issues of 'capacity' and 'leadership'. Pedagogy and curriculum are barely mentioned, other than references to the challenges of low levels of literacy and bilingual pupils (seen as a problem), with meagre understanding shown in either case. Relationships

[63]National Commission on Education, *Success Against the Odds: Effective Schools in Disadvantaged Areas* (London: Routledge, 1996). Despite the dominant message, this is a mixed text with a range of voices. Only Macbeath's chapter refers substantially to curriculum and pedagogy, but there are good examples of curricula which provide a broad cultural experience, including the arts and outdoor activities; a recurrent emphasis on building self-esteem; and attempts to reframe the emphasis on discipline in terms of self-discipline and respect. The authors of one chapter even develop a more political sense of 'setting high expectations' in terms of 'a belief that all children can succeed; that education is a vehicle for the emancipation of working-class children; that equality of opportunity is an absolute entitlement' (63).

[64]Margaret Maden, ed., *Success Against the Odds: Five Years On* (London: RoutledgeFalmer, 2001).

[65]Louise Stoll and Kate Myers, *No Quick Fixes: Perspectives on Schools in Difficulty* (London: Routledge, 1998).

[66]Paul Clarke, ed. *Improving Schools in Difficulty* (London: Continuum, 2005); Alma Harris, Judith Gunraj, Sue James, Paul Clarke and Belinda Harris, *Improving Schools in Exceptionally Challenging Circumstances – Tales from the Frontline* (London: Continuum, 2006); Mel Ainscow and Mel West, eds., *Improving Urban Schools – Leadership and Collaboration* (Maidenhead, UK: Open University Press, 2006); John MacBeath, Jane Cullen, David Frost and John Gray, *Schools on the Edge: Responding to Challenging Circumstances* (London: Chapman, 2007).

[67]David Reynolds (in Stoll and Myers, *No Quick Fixes*, 166) argues that that white children become threatened and consequently indulge in racial abuse and abuse when more than a third of the pupils in a school are from ethnic minorities; that Asian and white governors engage in 'racial conflicts' and are 'unable to give a unified response' when told by inspectors that the school is failing to provide an adequate education.

and ethos within the school are discussed with a disciplinary emphasis, in either a harder (traditional schooling) or a softer (Foucauldian) sense.

The neglect of the lives of students, their parents and neighbours shows the extent to which School Improvement has mirrored School Effectiveness at a deep level, despite the methodological differences. It is even more remarkable when we recall a comment made just a few years earlier by one of the editors, Kate Myers, referring critically to the prevalent *equiphobia*.[68] I am reminded once more of Angus' comment:

> Family background, social class, any notion of context are typically regarded as 'noise', as 'outside background factors' which must be controlled for and then stripped away so that the researcher can concentrate on the important domain of school factors.[69]

Angus is not saying here that school effectiveness studies overlook socio-economic factors. Indeed, proxy indicators of poverty[70] such as Free School Meal entitlement are regularly factored into calculations about the relative effectiveness of schools. More precisely, I believe, he is arguing that, once they have been utilised to provide fairer comparisons, they are effectively pushed aside in favour of a concentration on factors internal to the school. The same can be argued for most School Improvement studies in the English context, even those which focus on schools in areas of poverty.

This deep similarity, in terms of the acontextuality of both School Effectiveness and School Improvement, illustrates the importance, when examining paradigms, of seeing below the level of methodology. This silencing stands in stark contrast to books such as Pat Thomson's *Schooling the Rustbelt Kid*, Richard Riddell's *Schools for Our Cities*, or the work of American educators such as Lois Weis, Michelle Fine and colleagues.[71]

Social 'background' (the word is itself significant) is almost invisible in the recent books by Harris et al. and Ainscow and West (editors) – and we must remember that these are the very rare books within School Improvement which are dedicated to 'schools in challenging circumstances'. MacBeath et al. have published a more oppositional account of the same research project, which includes a more solid and contextualised description of pupils' lives.[72]

In a Kuhnian sense, schools struggling in areas of poverty represent a large 'anomaly', i.e. a stumbling block, an unfortunate piece of reality which causes us to question the adequacy of an established paradigm. They should lead us to question its basic entities and relationships, i.e. whether our centre of attention should be the (supposedly) self-managing school qua organisation, as a basic entity, or whether we should be focusing more on the relationship between school-as-community and its students' wider communities (neighbourhood, class,

---

[68]Kate Myers, 'Review of "Equal Opportunities in the New Era"', *Education* 5 (October 1990): 295.
[69]See note 33 above.
[70]The methodological flaw should be noted that disadvantage indicators may help to explain low attainment, but not be so closely tied to markers of high attainment. There may be a much stronger positive correlation between, let us say, mothers with degrees and children gaining A-levels than the negative correlation between free meals and A-levels. We should also note the problem of 'bipolar distribution', i.e. that some schools with large numbers of children on free meals may also have a large number of professional graduate parents.
[71]Pat Thomson, *Schooling the Rustbelt Kids: Making the Difference in Changing Times* (Stoke-on-Trent, UK: Trentham, 2002); Richard Riddell, *Schools for Our Cities: Urban Learning in the 21st Century* (Stoke-on-Trent, UK: Trentham, 2003); Lois Weis and Michelle Fine, eds., *Construction Sites: Excavating Race, Class and Gender among Urban Youth* (New York: Teachers College Press, 2000); Lois Weis and Michele Fine, eds., *Beyond Silenced Voices: Class, Race, and Gender in United States Schools*, rev. ed. (New York: SUNY Press, 2005).
[72]See note 66 above for references.

culture). It raises questions about perspective, e.g. whether we regard the schools, the students and their families, in deficit mode, as 'struggling' exceptions within an otherwise functional system. It should also raise questions of knowledge boundaries – why most School Improvement authors seem so unaware of the other shelves of the education library – and of methodology.

There is no space here to expand an argument which I have developed elsewhere[73] beyond briefly summarising some of the common features found during fieldwork in successful inner-city schools:[74]

(1) A strong emphasis was given to core skills and particularly literacy, but within a rich and exciting curriculum with an emphasis on the arts, community events, and socially critical versions of citizenship education.
(2) The curriculum frequently showed respect for the parents' cultural heritage, but was not limited to this, and opportunities were found for learners to reflect on cultural change and difference, as well as issues of power.
(3) Social constructivist pedagogies were very frequent, with an emphasis on co-operative problem-solving and investigation. These were carefully structured to ensure exploration and consolidation of deep concepts, to stimulate critical thinking, and to ensure language development. The rich multisensory approach to learning helped connect abstract concepts to real experience.
(4) Rather than 'discipline' or 'behaviour', the recurrent word in these schools was 'respect', with its rich cultural resonance.
(5) Leadership was 'distributed' not in a narrow sense of delegation, but in terms of drawing on the insight and initiative of staff with strong community roots. Headteachers themselves had many community connections, and a kind of political defiance, rejecting all assumptions that students growing up in inner-city neighbourhoods were destined to fail.

By contrast, the mainstream School Improvement literature[75] appears stuck in a managerialist frame, which renders it particularly incapable of addressing the key issues for schools in areas of poverty. The paradigm creates a filter which affects what researchers see and focus upon.

The wider context is New Labour policy with regard to poverty, which is marked by considerable tensions. Stephen Ball has argued that education agenda is so much set by the desire for economic competitiveness that there is 'an increasing neglect or sidelining (other than in rhetoric) of the social purposes of education'.[76] Whilst New Labour politicians' expressions of concern with social justice may be genuine, they take second place to, and must fit the frame of, a dogmatic belief in neo-liberal economics.[77] The mainstream School Improvement paradigm is, I would argue, nested within this wider economic and political paradigm, and has been profoundly affected by it.

---

[73]Terry Wrigley, 'The Politics of Improvement: What Hope Now for Working-class Kids', in Clarke, *Improving Schools in Difficulty*; Terry Wrigley, 'Schools and Poverty: Questioning the Effectiveness and Improvement Paradigms', *Improving Schools* 9, no. 3 (2006): 273–90.
[74]Terry Wrigley, *The Power to Learn: Stories of Success in the Education of Asian and Other Bilingual Pupils* (Stoke-on-Trent, UK: Trentham, 2000).
[75]See, for example, Ainscow and West, *Improving Urban Schools*; Harris et al., *Improving Schools*; Christopher Chapman, *Improving Schools through External Intervention* (London: Continuum, 2005).
[76]Stephen Ball, *The Education Debate* (Bristol, UK: Policy Press, 2008), 11–12.
[77]Ibid., 153–92.

Neo-liberalism

School Improvement remains resolutely apolitical in its theory, despite having been raised to a level of enormous political importance. There is a silence about power, which does not of course either resist or remove the operation of power. As Lukes[78] has coherently argued, power is often strongest where it is invisible and unspoken. The tacit assumptions about school norms, reinforced by a complicity with government schemes of surveillance and control, sustains a tone of pragmatism and moderation which objectively colludes with injustice and inequality.

The neglect of power extends also to a failure to question *in whose interests* – essentially the question why School Effectiveness and School Improvement have been so readily accepted and promoted politically and administratively as the 'only show in town'. An alternative paradigm of educational reform must emphasise the two principles of social justice and democratic citizenship.

Ontologically this depends on a sense of class, in two different senses. Educational sociology relies heavily on an occupational distinction between manual workers and white collar/professional families, to explain children's different attainment levels. This has been extended by examining the additional difficulties resulting from poverty (and, though often seen as disconnected, 'race' and gender). It is essential to retain this focus, whilst at the same time considering a Marxist distinction between capitalists and workers, increasingly operating as forces on a global scale. The latter definition underpins the importance of defending schools as a site for citizenship education, in opposition to attempts to gear schools more closely to economic functions.

This sense of class also requires an understanding of neo-liberalism as a class ideology and practice (see David Harvey,[79] among others). Some recent studies seek to interpret educational reform in these terms, including (with reservations) Andy Hargreaves, and (more directly) Alan Sears and Stephen Ball.[80] Hargreaves begins to see through the policy rhetoric of the 'knowledge society'; he argues that large sections of the population work at low-paid 'McJobs' to support the 'weightless' work of the 'knowledge economy', and increasingly their teachers are being retrained in very limiting ways through what he calls 'performance sects' rather than deep staff and school development. Sears argues that schooling today is being made to fit the needs of 'fast capitalism' in a slimmed down way, involving a reorientation towards basic skills and vocational training, and a socialisation of young people 'as self-commodifying individuals, prepared to take their place in the market as sellers of their own capacity to work (labour power)'.[81] Ball presents a scholarly analysis of privatisation as economic transformation and as discourse. He sees England as a 'laboratory of political transformation which exports policy solutions across the globe',[82] involving new ways of using the state as a 'commodifying agent'[83] to promote new opportunities for private enterprise under the shield of 'partnership'.

---

[78]Steven Lukes, *Power: A Radical View*, 2nd ed. (Basingstoke, UK: Palgrave Macmillan, 2005).
[79]David Harvey, *A Brief History of Neoliberalism* (Oxford: Oxford University Press, 2005).
[80]Andy Hargreaves, *Teaching in the Knowledge Society: Education in the Age of Insecurity* (Maidenhead, UK: Open University Press, 2003); Alan Sears, *Retooling the Mind Factory* (Aurora, ON: Garamond Press, 2003); Stephen Ball, *Education PLC: Understanding Private Sector Participation in Public Sector Education* (London: Routledge, 2007).
[81]Sears, *Retooling the Mind Factory*, 13.
[82]Ball, *Education PLC*, 5.
[83]Ibid., 5.

Both Sears[84] and Ball[85] demonstrate how a manufactured 'crisis' of the public sector serves to create a 'necessarian logic' to privatisation.[86] The culture of performativity is 'insatiable'; it:

> changes meaning; it delivers re-design and ensures 'alignment'. It objectifies and commodifies public sector work; the knowledge work of educational institutions is rendered into 'outputs', 'levels of performance' and 'forms of quality', that is this process of objectification contributes more generally to the possibility of thinking about social services like education as forms of production, as 'just like' services of other kinds and other kinds of production' ... They are standardised, calculated, qualified and compared. More generally performativity works to edge public sector organisations into a convergence with the private sector.[87]

In chapter 6, 'Selling Improvement/Selling Policy/Selling Localities', he demonstrates how demands for 'continuous improvement' enable companies, in prospectuses which are 'breathlessly enthusiastic',[88] to offer:

> 'solutions', 'holistic change', 'vision', 'customised change', 'values-led approaches', 'creative challenges' and repeatedly 'transformation' to schools and education authorities.[89]

It is no longer tenable to discuss school improvement in the English context without recognising its entanglement with a neo-liberal project of privatisation.

The relationship between contemporary school reforms and neo-liberalism is complex and does not submit to any reductionist one-to-one matching. It requires a well-developed critical sociology of policy, and internationally the analysis is still embryonic. Nevertheless some features have a direct relevance to understanding the School Effectiveness/School Improvement paradigms and their possible future development:

- the argument that test scores will attract investment, in a situation where national governments are felt to have little leverage;
- the use of 'league tables' to generate a quasi-market, and subsequently their deployment within a more radical privatisation process;
- the accountability discourse as a means of fostering instrumental attitudes;
- the avoidance of any debate about educational values and purpose;
- the increasing reduction of primary education to 'basic skills' and of secondary to vocational preparation.[90]

There is some historical continuity here. As I have argued elsewhere, there is a fundamental contradiction in the relationship between capitalism and schooling: 'Capitalism needs workers who are clever enough to be profitable, but not wise enough to know what's really going on'.[91]

In a context of global crises – environmental (global warming), economic (debt, development, poverty) and military (war in the Middle East, the arms trade) – there is a drive not

---

[84]Sears, *Retooling the Mind Factory*, 4.
[85]Ball, *Education PLC*, 4.
[86]Watson and Hay (2003), cited in Ball, *Education PLC*, 33.
[87]Ball, *Education PLC*, 27–8.
[88]Ibid., 137.
[89]Ibid., 138.
[90]From Terry Wrigley, *Another School Is Possible* (London: Bookmarks, 2006), 18–19.
[91]Ibid., 8.

only to vocationalise secondary schooling, but also to minimise opportunities to develop an in-depth critical understanding among students. This trend has become increasingly obvious in official documents.[92]

Looking forward

It is difficult to speculate on the future of School Improvement in the English context,[93] given a determination to transfer many schools to privatised management (academies and trust schools). Ball's analysis[94] points strongly towards improvement (and near synonyms such as 'innovation', 'transformation') as a marketable commodity to be sold to schools from outside. Of course this new policy direction, or rather next step in neo-liberal reform, is not inevitable, and there is considerable resistance.

Much depends on whether teachers are able to see beyond present modes of schooling and can organise to transcend them. Under these conditions, it would be possible to utilise some of the earlier gains of School Improvement in terms of understanding collegial change processes, whilst re-connecting to a wider educational knowledge.[95] Whether or not this continues to be known as 'School Improvement', we would in effect have a different paradigm, more closely resembling earlier, less compromised versions.

It would be naïve to imagine that progressive educators can simply adopt innovative practices from other parts of the world. Nevertheless, in a situation where particular practices and discourses have become hegemonic, international examples of successful innovation are important.[96] These include consideration of curriculum and school reforms including the American networks. It is also important to note some change of mood – a desire for a more satisfying curriculum – expressed in small-scale experiments in England.[97]

However, it remains important to consider the deep structure of the dominant paradigm, and to outline a desired alternative which would enable a greater focus on social justice and democratic citizenship, as well as ensuring more successful learning and a healthier personal and social development. The following points and (for comparison with Table 1) a summary in Table 2 sketch some possibilities.

---

[92]Department for Education and Skills (DfES), *Five Year Strategy for Children and Learners* (London: DfES, 2004); DfES, *Higher Standards, Better Schools for All: More Choice for Parents and Pupils* (London: DfES, 2005); DfES, *Education and Inspection Act* (London: DfES, 2006).

[93]Some of the key figures in School Improvement in England in the formative years of the 1990s have refocused much of their attention on issues relating to the personal welfare of young people in schools (e.g. Kathryn Riley), or on more innovative or communitarian examples of school change (e.g. Michael Fielding), whilst John MacBeath in particular has sought to reconnect with more progressive versions of School Improvement in Europe and elsewhere. Despite some new acolytes pursuing School Improvement as a kind of 'normal science', in Kuhn's terminology, the central core is smaller. This is not to suggest that the paradigm is of less account, since it has become institutionalised through bodies such as the National College of School Leadership and the influence of government agencies on schools and education authorities.

[94]Ball, *Education PLC*, 135–46.

[95]An interesting model for such a reworking of concepts such as learning community, leadership and professional development is provided by Debra Hayes, Martin Mills, Pam Christie and Bob Lingard, *Teachers and Schooling Making a Difference: Productive Pedagogies, Assessment and Performance* (Sydney: Allen and Unwin, 2006).

[96]Wrigley, *Schools of Hope*; Wrigley, *Another School Is Possible*.

[97]Current examples include the NESTA Future Lab project sponsored by the RSA (Royal Society of Arts); and the increasing appeal to 'creativity'. The *Children's Plan*, a diffuse and contradictory policy statement, admits the need for a bigger emphasis on play. DCFS (Department for Children, Schools and Families), *The Children's Plan: Building Brighter Futures* (London, 2007).

Table 2. Summary of principal characteristics of an alternative paradigm.

Entities, forces, laws (ontological)	The school as a community within a wider community, the dynamics of which derive from the daily passage of students between the two and staff responses to this.
Models and theories	A model of change built on pedagogical and sociological knowledge, including critical organisation theory.
Legitimate problems and acceptable solutions	An overwhelming orientation to learners' engagement and social development, with a focus on social justice and democratic citizenship, with capacity raised by collaborative evaluation by participants.
Methods and instruments	An emphasis on processes of participatory evaluation, including dialogue with the wider community. Learning from and piloting alternative practices, monitoring the development and achievement of less successful students. Participant research drawing upon pedagogical theory and ethnographies of social interaction.
Political frames	A preparedness to challenge external regulations and wider social policies where they conflict with principles of social justice and global citizenship.
Ethical considerations	A preparedness to engage in debate about curricular aims, pedagogical practices and organisational norms, in relation to the school's contribution to community development and wider social and environmental issues.

- *Entities and forces/relationships*: looking at schools as communities within wider communities, and the problematic movements of young people between these different cultures.
- *Models or theories*: drawing on sociological thinking which casts light on this experience, for example Bourdieu's theories of exchange and in/validation (cultural and social capital).
- *Field (the range of problems and acceptable solutions)*: a wider understanding of educational outcomes than test results, and a breadth of vision taking in curriculum and pedagogy, school ethos and community links, as well as change processes.
- *Methodology*: engaging in more sophisticated and critical forms of qualitative enquiry, drawing for example on traditions of ethnography such as symbolic interactionism.[98]
- *Political dimensions*: seeking to relate school-level developments to wider economic, social and cultural changes, in particular neo-liberalism and globalisation, as well as a critical discussion of national policy directives.

[98]A good account is provided by Herbert Blumer, *Symbolic Interactionism: Perspective and Method* (Berkeley: University of California Press, 1969). Goffman provides an even stronger model by applying such principles within strongly normative institutional contexts, and exploring the function of acting a role. For example, Charles Lemert and Ann Branaman, eds., *The Goffman Reader* (Oxford: Blackwell, 2006).

- *Ethical dimensions*: engaging in debate about curricular aims, the social benefits and implications of alternative forms of school organisation and modes of learning, and the contribution of schools towards community development, sustainability, peace, democracy and social justice.

Teaching educational leadership and administration in Australia

Richard Bates and Scott Eacott

Introduction

The teaching of educational leadership and administration in Australia is quite widespread, some 22 of the 36 universities offering units or programmes. It also has a long history, beginning in the 1950s at the universities of Queensland and New England. Academics from Australian universities have also made significant contributions to the international literature of the field. Given this amount of activity it would seem reasonable to ask if there is a long-standing tradition, an 'Australian perspective', that would inform teaching in the field or whether the field has indeed become 'global'. There has, however, been little investigation of what is actually taught in university programmes, whether it constitutes a coherent perspective or 'voice' or how that voice is incorporated into a global approach to the field. This article examines, firstly, the material used in teaching the field in Australia and, secondly, the contribution made by Australian scholars to the international literature in leading journals.

Two publications in particular stimulated the agenda for this article. In the first, Pat Thomson[1] examined a key Australian practitioner journal (*The Practising Administrator*, now published as *The Australian Educational Leader*) as a source of the professional definition of principals' work, concluding that there was an overwhelming emphasis on

---

[1] Pat Thomson, 'How Principals Lose Face', *Discourse: Studies in the Cultural Politics of Education* 22, no. 1 (2001): 5–22.

'operational and technical matters' while issues of policy, curriculum and pedagogy were notable by their absence.[2] Moreover, 'pictures of principals as embodied moral subjects dealing with complex and shifting situations' were completely absent.[3] In the second, Bill Mulford provided *An Overview of Research on Australian Educational Leadership 2001–2005* and concluded that there was a quite limited research literature on leadership which constituted only 10–14% of published articles in four key Australian journals.[4]

As there are significant numbers of leaders and aspiring leaders undertaking programmes in educational administration and leadership across Australia, the question of what they are being taught is an important issue. Are programmes focused on Thomson's 'operational and technical matters' or are they founded in the limited published research discovered by Mulford? Have they yet developed a concern with policy, curriculum and pedagogy? Do they now regard school leaders as 'embodied moral subjects dealing with complex and shifting situations?'

This article attempts an initial assessment of what resources are currently being used to teach educational leadership and administration in Australia and explores the sources, themes and characteristics of the field as represented in textbooks, journals and readings in use in some 15 of the key institutions that responded to my request for copies of their reading lists. The data therefore incorporates material from two-thirds of the programmes offered by large and small, metropolitan and regional universities in all states.

Some caveats must also be entered. The reading lists are in quite different formats and are not always easily comparable. Some references were incomplete or inaccurate and were therefore discarded. Some institutions provided broad reference lists rather than required reading lists: some were so extensive as to provide an almost complete bibliography of the field and were clearly not meant as prescribed reading.[5] Such lists were used selectively and references included only where there was evidence that particular sources were required reading. Other lists provided references to material that was concerned with highly specialised fields. General units in research methods were excluded from the list. There is clearly an arbitrary nature to some of these decisions, but they seem to have had little distorting effect on the findings of the survey as a whole.

Across the 15 institutions 53 separate offerings[6] were identified and included in the current study. Commonly, institutions offered up to four units within an educational leadership and administration specialisation with only three institutions offering more than four options within the field.

This article considers three main sources of teaching materials: textbooks, journal articles and extracts from books. Some institutions are clearly using websites and on-line journals as sources of readings. These are not, as yet, extensively in use but indicate a transition in source material that will be included in a later version of the article.

Textbooks

The most obvious feature of the survey was that the prescription of textbooks seems to have gone out of fashion. Only seven of the 15 institutions prescribe textbooks in 12 of the 53 units. Of the 35 textbooks listed 15 were published in the USA, 10 in the UK and 10 in Australia.

---

[2] Ibid., 7.
[3] Ibid., 5.
[4] Bill Mulford, *An Overview of Research on Australian Educational Leadership 2001–2005* (Winmallee, NSW: Australian Council for Educational Leaders, 2007).
[5] One such list for a single semester unit contained 32 books; more than two per week.
[6] Units of work.

Only three textbooks were used by more than one institution. One was American (Starratt, 2004) and two were Australian (Limerick et al., 2002 and Lingard et al., 2003). Notably, texts that were once standard, such as Hoy and Miskel's *Educational Administration: Theory, Research and Practice* (2001), are no longer a feature of textbook lists, the current edition being used by only one institution. Only two publishers (Allen & Unwin (four) and Open University Press (three)) had more than two texts listed, while seven publishers (Lawrence Erlbaum, McGraw Hill, NCSL, Paul Chapman, Teachers College Press, Thomson and Jacaranda-Wiley) had two texts listed; 75% of the texts were published in the last five years and none was more than a decade old.

Textbooks are no longer the main source of material in Australian courses on educational leadership and administration. It also seems clear that there is no consistent pattern in their usage. Moreover, while there is a slight predominance of American texts (15), both British (10) and Australian (10) texts are in use. There is little commonality in text adoption across institutions.

Book sections

If textbooks have gone out of fashion, then readings taken from single and multiple authored books have become very fashionable, perhaps because of the relative ease of copying resulting from new technologies and copyright laws which permit limited copying for research purposes. Across the 53 units some 243 chapters or sections from books were prescribed reading.

While multiple multi-national publishing locations and publishing conglomerates make national identification somewhat difficult, the major sources of publication were the UK (84 readings), the USA (73), Australia (38) and Europe (24). The dominant publishers were Springer (now including Elsevier and Kluwer, 24), RoutledgeFalmer (20), Sage (19), Jossey-Bass (12), Paul Chapman (10) and Open University Press (10), with Allen & Unwin, Cassell, Macmillan, Oxford University Press and Wiley contributing seven each. Surprisingly, given their relevance to the Australian context, only one publication from the Australian Council of Educational Leaders (ACEL) and one from the Australian Council for Educational Research (ACER) appeared on the list.

The most widely used sources of such extracts were the *International Handbook of Educational Change* (Hargreaves et al., 1998: 14 readings) followed some way back by the *Dynamics of Organizational Change and Learning* (Boonstra, ed., 2004: five readings): then *Leadership in Crisis?* (Ehrich and Knight, 1998), and *Organisational Effectiveness and Improvement* (Harris et al., 1998), four each; then, *Developing Teacher Leaders* (Crowther et al., 2002), *Educational Administration: Theory, Research and Practice* (Hoy and Miskel, 2001), *Shaping School Culture* (Deal and Petersen, 1999) and *The Essentials of School Leadership* (Davies, 2005) at three each.

Across the full range of 243 extracts only one author's writings were used 10 times (Fullan), with Fink, Hargreaves, and Starratt being used four times each and Angus, Blasé, Bush, Crowther, Deal and Petersen, Gronn, Hoy and Miskel, Mulford, Schein, and Silins being used three times each. These 14 authors accounted for some 12% of the 164 authors cited. Some 150 authors were used only once or twice.

In order to determine the topics covered by these readings, titles, key-words, and unit titles were used to provide a rough classification of content. The overwhelmingly most common topic was Educational Change (46/243), a dominance that was further enhanced if combined with Organizational Change (17). Next in frequency came Educational Policy (19), Organizational Theory (19), Educational Leadership (18), Ethics and School Leadership (16),

Organisational Learning (13), Professional Development (11), Collaborative Leadership (10), Leadership and Gender (eight), School Culture; School Effectiveness and Improvement; and Strategic Leadership (seven each) and Leadership and Globalization (six). Other than Educational Change, no topic was represented by more than 10% of the readings. Emotional Management (three), School Choice (three), and Financial and Legal Management (two) were addressed by single institutions.

The highest proportions of literature for particular topics came from particular publishing sources. For instance, Collaborative Leadership was dominated by readings published in the USA; Educational Change by Europe and the UK; Educational Leadership by the UK; Educational Policy by Australia and the UK; Ethics and School Leadership by the UK and the USA; Leadership and Gender by the UK; Leadership Theory by the USA; Organizational Change by the USA; Organizational Culture by the USA; Organizational Learning by the UK and the USA; Organizational Theory by the UK; School Culture by the USA; School Effectiveness and Improvement and Strategic Leadership by the UK. Australian contributions were concentrated in Educational Policy, Organizational Change and Professional Development, although if Australian authors published overseas, such as Crowther et al. (USA) and Gronn (UK), were reassigned, significant contributions were made to Collaborative Leadership and Educational Leadership, respectively.

Overall, the impression is one of considerable eclecticism. While there is some agreement on the dominant themes, the sources of readings relating to those themes remain widely dispersed in terms of authors, publishers and location of publication, with only one area (Educational Policy) where anything approaching a majority of extracts are Australian. Significantly, important sources of Australian monographs such as the ACER and ACEL are notable for their absence.

Readings from journals

If Australian programmes in Educational Leadership and Administration are enthusiastic about selecting readings from books, then they are even more enthusiastic about readings from journals, where 362 papers are spread across the 53 units offered by the 15 institutions.

The *International Journal of Educational Management* was overwhelmingly the most popular source with some 33 or nearly 10% of readings,[7] followed by *The Journal of Educational Administration* (20), *The Practising Administrator/The Australian Educational Leader* (17), *The Journal of Education Policy* (15), *School Leadership and Management* (14), *The Harvard Business Review* (13), *Leading and Managing* (12), *The International Journal of Leadership in Education* (12), *Educational Leadership* (10), *Educational Management, Administration and Leadership* (10) and *Educational Administration Quarterly* (10). These 11 journals account for over 45% of readings, while the remaining 55% were spread over some 134 journal titles with no other journal contributing more than six papers. Interestingly, while American journals dominate so many scholarly fields, five of these 11 journals are published in the UK: four by Falmer and one by Sage. Three journals are published in the USA and three in Australia, two by the Australian Council for Educational Leaders.

Once again, using key-words, paper titles and unit titles the 362 readings can be grouped into a dozen major themes: Educational Change (46), Organisational Leadership and Learning (46), Collaborative Leadership (32), Professional Development, Supervision and Mentoring (30), Leadership and Organizational Theory (30), Ethics, Leadership and Social

[7]Although this figure may be skewed by one unit that used almost no other sources.

Justice (25), Strategic Leadership and Planning (19), School Effectiveness, Improvement and Reform (19), Leadership and Gender (16), Leadership and Globalisation (15), Difference and Diversity (14), Leader Careers (nine), Educational Policy (eight), Accountability (seven) and School Culture (seven).

Authorship was, once again, widely dispersed, with no author represented by more than 10 papers – even where first authors of collaborative papers were included. Only three authors were represented more than five times: Mulford (nine), Cranston (eight) and Hargreaves (six). Only 15 further authors were represented by more than three papers: Bottery (five), Senge (five), Thomson (four), Leithwood (four), Drucker (four), Dimmock (four), Davies (four), Angus (three), Argyris (three), Blackmore (three), Calabrese (three), Hallinger (three), Harris (three), Muijs (three) and Silins (three). Of these 18 authors seven are Australian, seven American, and four British, although there is often collaboration across borders, as in the case of Mulford, Leithwood and Silins.

Of the 362 journal articles, 132 are less than five years old, 137 between five and 10 years old and 93 more than 10 years old, some of them classics in the field.

As with the readings from books, readings from journals are eclectic and diverse, both in source and author, but coalesce around a limited number of topics, even if the selection of authors does not coalesce in a similar way. British and Australian journals predominate in the main sources although in the more widespread variety of other journals a significant number of US journals are represented, though seldom by more than one or two papers.

Overall themes and sources

Not surprisingly the top 10 themes that emerge from book sections and journal readings overlap very considerably. However, somewhat different emphases in type of source change the overall ranking of thematic priorities as Table 1 shows.

Overall it seems clear that there is some commonality in major themes within the field of educational leadership and administration. Understanding, Managing and Leading Change has become the dominant theme. Organisational and Leadership Theory follows close behind. These themes are unsurprising and have been part of educational leadership and administration programmes for some time. The next three themes, however, seem to have emerged as more significant in such programmes in more recent years. Organisational

Table 1. Top 10 themes by book sections, journal papers and when combined.

	Book sections		Journal papers		Combined	
Theme	Number	Rank	Number	Rank	Number	Rank
Educational and organisational change	63	1	46	=1	109	1
Organisational and leadership theory	37	2	30	=4	67	2
Organisational learning	13	5	46	=1	59	3
Collaborative leadership	10	7	32	3	42	4
Ethics and leadership	16	4	25	6	41	=5
Professional development	11	6	30	=4	41	=5
Educational policy	19	3	8	9	27	7
School effectiveness and improvement	7	=9	19	=7	26	=8
Strategic leadership and planning	7	=9	19	=7	26	=8
Leadership and gender	8	8	16	8	24	10

Learning, Collaborative Leadership, and Ethics and Educational Leadership are topics that have gained considerably more attention during the past decade. Professional Development might also be argued to have emerged as a priority in successful leadership and as an essential component of School Effectiveness and Improvement. Educational Policy, and Strategic Leadership and Planning clearly present contextual understandings for the field. Gender issues in educational leadership and administration come quite low on the list, but at least they are there in a way that they perhaps were not a decade ago.[8]

If Thomson was concerned about the emphasis on 'operational and technical matters' in her assessment of the *Practising Administrator*'s definition of the principals' role and about the lack of emphasis on policy, learning and ethics, then perhaps this analysis indicates a willingness in those who teach educational administration to move towards a more academic and a more comprehensive definition of the field. When compared with the preoccupations of a decade or two ago, some changes do appear to have occurred.

In terms of Mulford's 73 references to Australian research on educational leadership, however, only 10 appeared anywhere on the reading lists, giving some support to his contention that not only is there a shortage of Australian research in the area, but that Australian researchers and teachers take little notice of it anyway. Again, if matched with the list of recommended reading attached to the Australian Principals Associations Professional Development Council Report *Leaders Lead: Beyond the Lost Sandshoe*,[9] none of the recommendations made there appear in textbook lists and only two of the recommendations appear on journal or book section lists. There is a similar lack of congruence with Watson's scan of research findings on quality teaching and leadership.[10]

Again, one might ask, whatever happened to those Australian writers in the field that contributed an Australian voice to the field internationally during the 1980s and 1990s: Angus, Bates, Beare, Begley, Blackmore, Burford, Caldwell, Chapman, Cranston, Crowther, Dempster, Dimmock, Dinham, Duignan, Evers, Gronn, Gurr, Keating, Kenway, Lakomski, Limerick, Lingard, Logan, Marginson, Mulford, Rizvi, Silins, Smyth, Teese, Thomson, Walker, among others? Of the 640 textbooks, book extracts and journal articles listed only one author gets more than 10 mentions (Mulford, 13); only five are mentioned five or more times (Angus, six; Crowther, six; Duignan, five; Gronn, five; Silins, six). It seems that the rich tradition of debate is hardly referred to in contemporary discussions of leadership and administration. It may be, of course, that the ideas developed by such scholars are incorporated into later writing. However, if this is so it would seem that there is little recourse to original source material.

So what are we to say about the teaching of educational leadership and administration in Australia? From the admittedly incomplete evidence presented here, there appears to be some consistency in the themes currently presented to students. It also seems to be the case that the teaching of these themes is derived from a very wide, eclectic reserve of American, British and Australian sources in both books and journals. Unlike book sections, journal papers are drawn from a more limited set of major journals, some 11 (mainly British and Australian) accounting for nearly half of the required readings.

---

[8]It is interesting to note the differences between this list and that employed in an American survey of principal leadership programmes which were: managing for results, managing personnel, technical knowledge, external leadership, norms and values, managing classroom instruction, and leadership and school culture. Frederick Hess and Andrew Kelly, 'Learning to Lead: What Gets Taught in Principal-preparation Programs', *Teachers College Record* 109, no 1. (2007): 244–74.

[9]Australian Principals Associations Professional Development Council (APAPDC), *Leaders Lead: Beyond the Lost Sandshoe* (Hindmarsh, South Australia: APAPDC, 2003).

[10]Louise Watson, *Quality Teaching and School Leadership* (Canberra: Teaching Australia, 2005).

However, little attention is paid to even the small amount of relevant Australian research. Finally, current teaching takes little account of preceding generations of scholarly work produced by Australian authors, few of whom figure prominently in the use of textbooks, book extracts or journal articles. Maybe it is time for us to start talking to each other about both research and teaching.

It is, of course, possible that the study and teaching of educational leadership and administration has become global to such an extent that local literature and traditions are less relevant. If this is so then it would be reasonable to expect that, as well as drawing predominantly on the global literature in the field, Australian authors would be found publishing widely within the global literature. In order to examine this possibility an audit of publications by Australian-based academics was conducted.

Auditing the Australian voice

To compile the data for analysis in this audit, the table of contents of each issue of leading educational administration and leadership journals were searched for the period 1977–2007. Unlike other fields (for example, MacMillian's[11] work in the field strategy), there currently exists no list of leading journals for educational leadership. Mayo et al.[12] produced a list entitled 'Which Journals Are Educational Leadership Professors Choosing?', however, the list contained both refereed and professional journals, and only those from the USA. To overcome this situation, early analysis of the 'Journal Banding study' conducted by the Centre for the Study of Research Training and Impact (SORTI) at the University of Newcastle, Australia, and the Australian Association for Research in Education (AARE) was used. In this study, over 900 education journals were identified. The journals were broken into 26 different fields. The most appropriate field for this audit was 'Administration, leadership, educational management and policy'. It consisted of 49 journals (see Table 2). For each journal a QScore (quality score) was calculated from three sources of information; survey responses (esteem measures, $N = 628$, 83% Australian, 82% employed by universities), the journal's ISI score (if it had one) and whether the journal has an international editorial board (for more information on the study see http://www.newcastle.edu.au/centre/sorti/).

To make the list workable, it was decided to reduce the list to the top 20 journals. The highest scoring journal in the field was the *Journal of Education Policy* with a QScore of 18.56. The five highest scoring journals in the discipline were the *American Educational Research Journal* (29.33), *British Educational Research Journal* (29.30), *Review of Educational Research* (29.21), *Teachers College Record* (28.54) and *Harvard Educational Review* (26.04). While being number one in the field, the *Journal of Education Policy* was ranked 56th overall in the discipline. This would be consistent with the work of others who have suggested that educational leadership has a relatively weak quality profile within the already weak quality profile of educational research.[13] However, it is to

[11] Ian MacMillian, 'The Emerging Forum for Business Policy Scholars', *Strategic Management Journal* 12 (1991): 161–5. Previous versions of the same analysis appeared in *Strategic Management Journal* in both 1990 and 1989.

[12] Russell Mayo, Perry Zirkel, and Brian Finger, 'Which Journals Are Educational Leadership Professors Choosing?', *Educational Administration Quarterly* 42, no. 5 (2006): 806–11.

[13] Dan Griffiths, *Administrative Theory in Transition* (Victoria, Australia: Deakin University, 1985); Steven Gorard, 'Current Contexts for Research in Educational Leadership and Management', *Educational Management Administration and Leadership* 33, no. 2 (2005): 155–64.

Table 2. Educational administration and leadership journals from SORTI/AARE study.

Journals	QScore	Location
Journal of Education Policy	18.56	UK
International Journal of Educational Management	15.84	UK
Educational Administration Quarterly	15.74	USA
Educational Management, Administration and Leadership	15.31	UK
Journal of Educational Administration	15.31	Australia
School Effectiveness and School Improvement	14.10	The Netherlands
Journal of Higher Education Policy and Management	14.08	Australia
Educational Policy	13.95	USA
International Journal of Leadership in Education	13.31	USA
School Leadership and Management	12.37	UK
The Australian Educational Leader	12.30	Australia
Journal of Educational Change	12.01	The Netherlands
Education Policy Analysis Archives	11.61	USA
Educational Evaluation and Policy Analysis	11.61	USA
Educational Leadership	10.53	USA
International Studies in Educational Administration	10.14	Cyprus
Policy Futures in Education	10.14	UK
Leading and Managing	9.70	Australia
International Electronic Journal for Leadership in Learning	9.52	Canada
Journal of Educational Administration and History	9.52	UK

Note: A further 29 journals were identified in the study with scores ranging from 9.36 to 0.00.

be noted that the *Journal of Education Policy* was ranked second (behind *Oxford Review of Education*) in a ranking study conducted in the UK by Wellington and Torgerson.[14]

The *International Journal of Educational Management* was not included in the field in the SORTI/AARE study. Rather it was included in the field of 'Economics, accounting, business and management'. The decision to include it in this audit was based on the fact that the journal featured prominently in the earlier stage of this study and in Eacott's[15] discourse analysis on the use of the term strategy in education. Seven of the 20 journals are published in the USA. The UK and Australia publish five and four, respectively. Two are from the Netherlands and one from both Canada and Cyprus. Interestingly no journals from the sub-continent or Asia (such as the *Journal of Educational Planning and Administration* – India) appear in the SORTI/AARE list.

Using the journals identified in Table 2, the tables of contents were searched for original articles (book reviews, editorial comments and research notes were excluded) where one of the authors was affiliated with an Australian educational institution. Despite appearing in the SORTI/AARE study, articles from *The Australian Educational Leader* and *Educational Leadership* were omitted because they had not been subject to peer-review processes. Having established the criteria for inclusion, a final sample of 981 articles out of a total of

[14]Jerry Wellington and Carole Torgerson, 'Writing for Publication: What Counts as a High Status, Eminent Academic Journal?', *Journal of Further and Higher Education* 29, no. 1 (2005): 35–48.
[15]Scott Eacott, 'An Analysis of Contemporary Literature on Strategy in Education', *International Journal of Leadership in Education* (forthcoming). Currently available at online first, http://dx.doi.org/10.1080/13603120701462111.

8521 were identified (11.51% of published works). Several patterns emerge from the data. Three journals standout as the dominant outlets for publication: *Leading & Managing* (*N* = 66, 58.93%), *Journal of Higher Education Policy and Management* (*N* = 249, 50.40%) and the *Journal of Educational Administration* (*N* = 209, 28.59%). No other journal has greater than 13.98% of articles written by Australian-based authors. Not surprising is that all three of these journals are based at Australian universities (Southern Queensland, Monash and Wollongong, respectively). If we remove these journals from the data, Australian authors are associated with 446 out of a total of 7184 articles, representing 6.21% of the sample. Although not holding a large percentage of published works, as a relatively small country (when compared with the population and economies of the USA and UK), it is possible to argue that Australia is fighting above its weight in the international literature.[16] In addition, educational leadership does not get the attention in Australia that it does receive in other nations such as the USA and UK.

All that being considered, the purpose of this audit in this article is to investigate whether or not there is a body of literature produced by Australian-based academics for educational administration educators to call on in their teaching. To attempt to answer this question, analysis was completed on the number of articles linked to Australian-based authors.

Figure 1 displays the percentage of articles linked to Australian-based authors in the time period 1977–2007. As would be expected in any such analysis, the percentage of publications experienced a series of ebbs and flows during the 30-year period. The peak result was in 1980, however only five journals were in operation at that time and two were

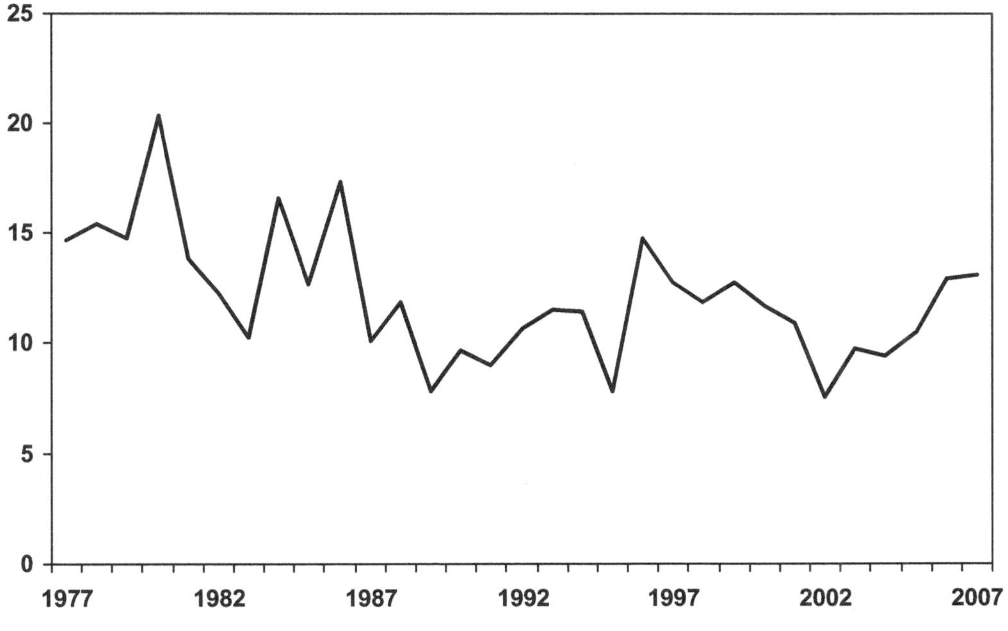

Figure 1. Percentage of articles by Australian-based academics in educational leadership journals.

[16]Richard Bates, 'Phelan's Bibliometric Analysis of the Impact of Australian Educational Research', *The Australian Educational Researcher* 30, no. 2 (2003): 57–64.

Table 3. Descriptive data of authorship over time.

Time period	Total articles	Total authors	Articles per author	Range	Single-article authors	Multiple-article authors	Leading author
1977–9	46	42	1.10	1–2	38	4	Many
1980–9	280	203	1.38	1–6	162	41	P.A. Duignan
1990–9	471	310	1.52	1–12	226	84	R.J.S. Macpherson
2000–7	610	386	1.58	1–21	291	95	B. Mulford
1977–2007	981	792	1.77	1–25	570	222	B. Mulford

housed in Australia. The lowest point was 2002 with 7.60%. The average percentage for the time period is 12.13% and the last two years have been 13.00%. Overall, the percentage of publications by Australian-based authors has remained relatively constant over time.

To further support this claim, the descriptive data from time periods was compared. Table 3 shows the descriptive data of authorship over time. Of particular interest was whether authors were making continued contributions or merely contributing one-off articles. Although the average number of articles per author has steadily increased over the last 30 years, it is still less than two and over 70% of authors contribute only one article. Furthermore to this situation, when viewing the sample from a first-author standpoint, 129 out of the 981 (13.1%) were based at Australian educational institutions that are not universities. While it is beyond the scope of this audit, it is proposed that many of these articles are written by research higher degree students based in schools. From reading this data, it is suggested that very few Australian authors are making a continued contribution to the existing body of knowledge in the field. The high prevalence of single contributions significantly limits the potential use of work in the teaching of educational administration and leadership.

It is not, however, all doom and gloom for the Australian educational administrative voice. While most authors have contributed few articles, a core group of academics have established a research track record. Table 4 shows the 10 most published authors in the time period 1977–2007. Not surprising, all bar one author had a publication period in excess of a decade (Macpherson is an exception).

Despite concerns raised in other works and the earlier phase of this study that the Australian educational leadership voice is diminishing, the data from this audit shows that the contribution of Australian-based authors in the field has remained constant over time. However,

Table 4. Most published authors, 1977–2007.

Author	Publication period	Associated articles
Mulford, B.	1984–2007	25
Gronn, P.	1982–2005	15
Dimmock C.	1987–2002	15
Wildy, H.	1992–2006	15
Macpherson, R.J.S.	1989–1996	14
McCormick, J.	1996–2007	14
Blackmore J.	1992–2006	12
Ehrich, L.C.	1994–2006	12
Smyth, J.	1977–2006	11
Duignan, P.	1980–2005	11

the Australian voice in the field has remained the domain of a few key contributors who publish in a limited number of journals. Many of the names (such as Mulford, Dimmock and Blackmore) overlap in the audit and readings for courses, although there are signs of a new group of scholars entering the dialogue (such as Ehrich, Wildy, Clarke, Cranston and McCormick). Arguably if this audit was done in 12 months' time more names may be added. The challenge for scholars in the field appears to be making a substantial contribution. Many write an article or two and disappear. Whether they pursue their research programmes in other fields is unknown.

This audit has taken a single lens to the contribution of Australians to the educational leadership voice. It is beyond the scope of this article to further elaborate on the wider range of questions being investigated in the audit. Many of these questions will be taken up in further works. Also to be noted is that many Australian are working in overseas institutions and continuing to make contributions to the wider field (for example, Begley and Walker). Additionally, this audit has only included publication outputs and not the impact of such publications. While a difficult process to undertake in the discipline of education, a further extension of this work may be to survey the perceived value or impact of publications by Australian authors. While providing valuable information in a quality assurance environment, such an investigation would also help to answer some of the questions surrounding the lack of building on and using Australian educational leadership work by fellow scholars.

Conclusion

This article set out to investigate the teaching of educational leadership and administration in the Australian context through course reading lists. The sample investigated demonstrated commonality in the themes addressed and shows a tendency for educators to adopt an academic (as opposed to operational) focus. However, despite a long and rich tradition, the use of Australian research and contributions by Australian-based academics were relatively limited. Initially this was thought to be a result of a decreasing presence of Australian-based academics in the field, but after conducting an audit of Australian contributions to the field's discourse, it appears to support Mulford's notion that Australian scholars and practitioners overlook each others' contributions, although it is unclear as to whether this is a deliberate or unintended action. But what does this mean for the teaching of educational leadership and administration in Australia?

For the educator, we suggest that courses be based in both the historical and contemporary discourse of the topic under discussion. This enables the student to develop an understanding of the topic with an appreciation of where the discussion has been and sets the foundations for where the discussion is heading next. As such, it is important to draw on both the local (Australian) and global contributions to the discussion to make informed conclusions. Contemporary (and arguably historical) discourse in the field argues for establishing a local perspective or context-specific interpretation of global issues, therefore why does the teaching of the field not adopt the same approach?

For the scholar, we suggest a greater focus on acknowledging the contributions of other Australians both past and present. This does not suggest that we want everyone to agree, rather, a more coherent discussion that takes into consideration the work of others and continues to move the field forward. Nobody, practitioner or scholar, benefits from a field that is littered with loosely related contributions that do not acknowledge one another. Contributions of this nature, while frequently interesting (although this could be debated elsewhere), offer little to the paradigmatic development of the field.

The teaching of educational leadership and administration in Australia is in a good position with many talented people working in the field. However, with the forthcoming turnover of staff (as in the majority of Western educational settings) in the educational leadership and administrative community of scholars, we would arguably benefit from listening and working with each other to further establish the unique Australian perspective within the global educational leadership and administration field. This would make our work as both educators and researchers of greater value within the global field.

Acknowledgements

The authors would like to acknowledge the research assistance provided by Yanping Lu (a doctoral student at the second author's institution) in the collection of the data for the audit of publication. Her tireless work was invaluable in getting this article prepared on time.

Modernisation and the field of educational administration

Helen M. Gunter

Introduction

Adams argues that public administration in the USA is a prisoner of modernity and as such it is concerned with scientific technical rationality.[1] Such knowledge claims are what underpinned the Theory Movement in the 1960s and 1970s in educational administration in western-style democracies.[2] The central concern was to produce a scientific and predictive theory of how organisations worked based on positive epistemology. This was challenged at the time, and as Greenfield states: 'many findings produced by the quantitative methods are dreams of the imagination asserted as the truth'.[3] While much is said about the 'new' and 'modern' in the contemporary education system, it seems to me that in England there is

---

[1]Guy B. Adams, 'Enthralled with Modernity: The Historical Context of Knowledge and Theory Development in Public Administration', *Public Administration Review* 52, no. 4 (1992): 1–22 (accessed through ProQuest, September 19, 2007).

[2]The Theory Movement in North America sought a scientific and unified approach to administration where facts and values are separated. See Dan E. Griffiths, ed., *Behavioural Science and Educational Administration. The 63rd Yearbook of the National Society for the Study of Education*, part II (Chicago: University of Chicago Press, 1964); Dan E. Griffiths, 'Intellectual Turmoil in Educational Administration', *Educational Administration Quarterly* 15, no. 3 (1979): 43–65; Andrew W. Halpin, ed., *Administrative Theory in Education* (London: Macmillan, 1958). In 1974 Tom Greenfield challenged the Theory Movement by arguing that organisations are not objective realities but exist within the subjective phenomenology of the individual as an invented social reality. He wrote about the reaction to this and the personal attacks on him: 'I have watched with surprise and fascination the furore which began with the presentation of my paper at the International Intervisitation Programme in 1974. I think it was, in Bristol. People ask me if the reaction bothers me. No it doesn't. The slings and arrows of academic warfare are not unpleasant. Somewhat like St Sebastian, I suppose, I'd rather be in pain as long as the crowd understands what the ceremony is about. But it is hard just to be written off, ignored or buried'. Tom Greenfield, 'Where Does Self Belong in the Study of Organisation? Response to the Symposium', *Educational Administration* 6, no. 1 (1978): 86–7.

[3]Tom Greenfield and Peter Ribbins, *Greenfield on Educational Administration* (London: Routledge, 1993), 237.

a danger of reinventing this Theory Movement through an obsession with delivery of targets, evidencing of performance, measuring the impact of headteachers as leaders on student outcomes[4] and presenting it as not only new but essentially correct.

An enduring epistemology remains. Adams cites the example of culture which seems a new and better way of understanding and improving public organisations, but he argues that organisational culture is a benign way of making the system work better rather than asking questions about wider social, political and economic cultures in which the organisation is located. How does this happen? Adams says it reminds him of the artist and the pentimento:

> Because canvas and stretcher bars are expensive, it has been a common practice for centuries for artists to paint over their earlier paintings in an effort to save money. Over the years, though, an image – a pentimento – from the earlier painting may bleed through what has been painted on top. Likewise, over the years, public administration theorists have painted new versions of public administration theories over the old, with the traditionalists …, the new public administration, and the interpretive and critical versions, all among them. Although each of these versions of public administration is thought of as affording an entirely new view of the field, the old images continue to bleed through. These old images – images of technique and rationality – are part and parcel of modernity, and they are not so easily covered over.[5]

I intend in this article to use the pentimento as a metaphor for examining the knowledge claims about the organisational arrangements for decisions about educational provision in England. In particular, while much is said about what is new and leading edge, in reality the dominance of hierarchy and centralisation bleeds through regarding the location and preferred exercise of power. I begin with the New Labour modernisation project, and focus specifically on Barber's account of reform implementation, and I critically examine the operation and limitations of such an approach. I go on to present a case for the production of histories about the past, for present practice and future aspirations. Underpinning this is the argument that if the modernisation agenda is about transformation, then historical analysis is key, because as Silver states: 'history is the recording and analysis of change – when, how and why it took place, or didn't'.[6]

The New Labour pentimento

New Labour modernisation is articulated through a change narrative where the language is one of modern, new, and improved. A totalising reconceptualisation producing a transformation of public services is promised based on: 'new roles, new work, new power relationships, new values and new employment'.[7] For example, Academy schools, funded by private philanthropists, are a product of the attack on state provision embodied in the comprehensive ideal, are growing in number but resistance remains in parts of the country. Indeed, the organisational arrangements for decision-making about educational services has faced major changes since 1944, some of which are highly significant and public such as the 1988 Education Reform Act where schools took on responsibilities for financial and human resources and relinquished responsibilities for determining the quality and content

[4]See Ken Leithwood and Ben Levin, *Assessing School Leader and Leadership Programme Effects on Pupil Learning* (London: Department for Education and Skills, 2005).
[5]Adams, 'Enthralled with Modernity', 12–13.
[6]Harold Silver, *Education, Change and the Policy Process* (Lewes, UK: The Falmer Press, 1990), 1.
[7]Helen M. Gunter and Graham Butt, 'Introduction: The Challenges of Modernization', in *Modernizing Schools: People, Learning and Organizations*, ed. Graham Butt and Helen Gunter (London: Continuum, 2007), 1.

of the curriculum.[8] Others are highly significant but surprisingly make little public impact such as the end of qualified teacher status (QTS) for headteachers and the use of teaching assistants who are not qualified teachers to teach children.

In this article I intend to focus on the New Labour modernisation project in England that is located in the activities of an 'alliance' of neo-liberals and neo-conservatives whose ideas and practice provided rationality for the previous Thatcherite administrations. Notably, New Labour has continued the attack on educational professionals and experts and the public provision of education, and strengthened the centralisation of decision-making about the curriculum, standards, and workforce training. While social justice remains a feature of Labour, with investment in early years, urban education, and schools in challenging circumstances, it is subject to the privatisation that has been a feature of both Conservative and Labour governments over the past 20 years. The main difference is that New Labour has been more regulatory in regard to how diversity and choice are to operate.

New Labour language is dramatic in its deliberate use of 'new', and 'modern' with 'pathfinder' and 'test bed' projects about the future visions of schools and schooling. The future is central to the modern, where New Labour claims to want to break with the past in order to resolve enduring problems that are affecting educational achievement. The narrative is around change where nothing less than complete transformation is acceptable. Hence the approach is not only restructuring with new systemic and local organisational arrangements but also reculturing where ways of thinking, working, and knowing about what must be done are to be learned. The approach is to: first, change the nature of what it means to be a professional educator, with an emphasis on being accountable for the performance of students and teaching assistants in the delivery of externally determined curricula through the use of ICT to access lesson plans and learning resources; second, change the nature of the school to a site for integrated children's services with provision for education, health, welfare and policing; third, change the composition and contribution of the workforce where those with QTS become just one group within children's services, and leadership is generic across services and organisations attracting those without QTS from the public, private and voluntary sectors to lead provision; fourth, change the culture and practice of provision through the adoption of private-sector practices (planning, target setting, auditing) and the employment of private-sector experts to deliver services such as financial managers, chief executives and data analysts. This is being driven by centralised regulation such as the 'Every Child Matters'[9] agenda combined with centralised performance management.

A useful way of examining this strategy is to examine Michael Barber's book, *Instruction to Deliver*,[10] where he outlines his time at Education,[11] and then as Director of Blair's Delivery Unit at No. 10. The emphasis in the first decade of New Labour has been on gathering data to prove that targets have been reached. This was necessary in order to keep middle-class voters (not least middle-class parents) on side in the massive funding of public-sector services. Barber and his team developed what became known as 'deliverology' and he shows its development and presents a manual outlining how to do it. It is underpinned by an imperative to ensure reforms determined centrally happen locally, and are sustained:

---

[8]In 2008 there will be a special edition of *Educational Management, Administration and Leadership* edited by Michael Strain and Tim Simkins to commemorate 20 years since the 1988 Education Reform Act.

[9]Department for Education and Skills (DfES), *Every Child Matters* (London: DfES, Cm 5860, 2003).

[10]Michael Barber, *Instruction to Deliver* (London: Politicos, 2007).

[11]The national ministry has been relabelled: Department for Education and Employment became the Department for Education and Skills.

> There are so many barriers to successful reform that one wonders sometimes how anyone ever achieves anything at all. It is not just the cynicism resulting from the track record that gets in the way. There is the tendency to have pleasant little projects which tinker at the edges of a service but do not change the core business. There is the ever present risk of watering down a proposal to gain consensus, with the result all too often that a roaring lion becomes a squeaking mouse. There is the risk that before a reform has really made a difference, the agenda shifts, attention is diverted elsewhere and the service slips back to its pre-existing state. Most of all, there is the danger of underestimating the extraordinary deadweight force of institutional inertia. No wonder most reforms fail, and I haven't yet mentioned the two barriers – bad ideas and gross incompetence – which are so obvious they would hardly need stating but for their historical pedigree. Remember the poll tax?[12]

Unpacking this begs two interconnected questions: Why are New Labour ideas good ideas, and what makes New Labour competent? What Barber is railing about is the legacy of history, and how waves of reforms lie over each other, interact, produce intended and unintended outcomes. His strategy for dealing with this is both conceptual and instrumental. Conceptually he has drawn on and reworks concepts such as accountability to mean answerability for target delivery, and he locates this in a language of modernisation such as ambition and transformation. Instrumentally, he works the system by: first, building a team of civil servants who are committed to his way of doing things; second, using micropolitics to ensure others (prime minister, permanent secretaries, Treasury) are on side and stay on side (the analogy with football and cricket dominates thinking and dispositions to practice in this text); third, building alliances outside of Whitehall with those who have a stake in New Labour, not least private-sector consultants and companies who can be contracted to deliver; and fourth, creating and supporting non-departmental public bodies (NDPBs) such as the National College for School Leadership (NCSL), in contractual relations with the private sector, to deliver.

The central problem for Barber is that for deliverology to work the voices and dialogue integral to liberal democracy need to be marginalised or silenced or brought on side. Hence teachers are ridiculed as producers who operate in their own self-interests, and academics are even worse because we will not do as we are told.[13] The deliverology process silences these voices through the operation of the 'delivery chain':

> The crucial concept is the delivery chain. Again, it is no more than a blinding flash of the obvious, but none the less important for all that. The best way to think about it is to imagine what is implicit when a minister makes a promise. Supposing that a minister promises, as David Blunkett did, to improve standards of reading and writing among eleven-year-olds. Implicit in this commitment is that, in one way or another, the minister can influence what happens inside the head of an eleven-year-old in, for example, Widnes. The delivery chain makes that connection explicit; so in this case, what is the connection between the child in Widnes and the minister in Westminster? What happens in side of that eleven-year-old's head is influenced chiefly by her teacher – the first link in the chain; the teacher is influenced by the school's literacy co-ordinator, who in turn is influenced by the headteacher – the second and third links in the chain. The headteacher is influenced by the governors and the local authority, who are influenced by the regional director of the National Literacy Strategy, who answers to the national director of the strategy. He in turn answers to the head of the Standards and Effectiveness Unit in the Department for Education, who answers to the secretary of state. And thus we have established the delivery chain.[14]

---

[12]Barber, *Instruction to Deliver*, 72.

[13]Barber states: 'Through all this I found myself learning how to manage not just officials, but also the system as a whole. After working in universities, my first impressions of departmental officials were positive – unlike academics, when asked to do something, they generally did it'. Barber, *Instruction to Deliver*, 33.

[14]Barber, *Instruction to Deliver*, 85.

Do note the interesting shift here from 'influence' to 'answer', and from the student as 'she' to the national director of the strategy as a 'he'.

Epistemologically this process assumes a direct cause and effect connection, where human encounters ensure an upwards process of accountability, and a downwards process of direction. This rational scientific linear model bleeds through the normative rhetoric of 'new' New Labour policy texts that claim to be based on values with a commitment to empowerment and a respect for professionals.[15] The minister impacts on the child's head regarding an instruction from national agencies to deliver on literacy and numeracy, but the child cannot engage in a dialogue about this. The emphasis in the delivery chain is to produce data on the child's performance, and then use that to judge the effectiveness of the adults who are proximate or distant to them (teacher or minister), and to problem solve where data can show patterns of outcome that require interventions. It seems that children do not have a personal history, the school they are in does not have a history, the community they live in does not have a history, and the means by which children, learning, professionals, communities, and national policy might be inter-connected differently through other ways of knowing and knowers, is not considered. Indeed the NCSL comes in for criticism because of its failure to operate correctly in the delivery chain:

> Most troubling of all was evidence that the training of headteachers by the NCSL for the Consultant Leaders' Programme had given little attention to literacy and numeracy and, indeed, a reading of the materials suggested that this seminal programme, instigated by a minister to improve performance in the national tests, had been heavily influenced by the purveyors of management gobbledegook who are always lurking in the education backwoods, waiting for their moment. Indeed, we had evidence that some of the trainers on the course had even made explicit the view that focusing on literacy and numeracy was actually wrong. My faith in the NCSL, and in the departmental officials whose job it should have been to check every detail of the training programme before it began, was shaken.[16]

This is illustrative of how the control of the chain is centralised, and how those who exercise voice or what used to be known as 'professional discretion' are ridiculed. This is not a new strategy, and 'show trials' in the media or the deliberate ignoring of research evidence that encourages debate is a feature that continues to bleed through.

The deliverology model has now become a product to be sold internationally, and in reflecting on this Barber asks the question: 'was deliverology moral?', and he comes to the conclusion that 'large parts of deliverology could be put to less worthy purposes'.[17] What is deemed worthy is a political decision, and the expectation in a liberal democracy is that options and evidence are open for ongoing dialogue. It seems to me that there is a banality in deliverology which is reminiscent of Arendt's[18] arguments about how people engaging in practice can be shaping and promoting forms of what I have called 'ordinary tyranny'.[19] This is forcefully put by Inglis:

---

[15]For example, look at the New Labour Green Paper from 1998, *Teachers: Meeting the Challenge of Change*, which presents the rhetoric of the modern professional who needs to be transformed and who needs to become transforming. This is the type of text that I have examined in Helen M. Gunter, *Rethinking Education: The Consequences of Jurassic Management* (London: Cassell, 1997), where I look at how knowledge production is related to the scientific rational model.

[16]Barber, *Instruction to Deliver*, 187.

[17]Ibid., 293.

[18]Hannah Arendt, *Eichmann in Jerusalem: A Report on the Banality of Evil* (Harmondsworth, UK: Penguin, 1977).

[19]Helen M. Gunter, 'Remodelling the School Workforce in England: A Study in Tyranny?', *Journal of Critical Education Policy Studies* 5, no. 1 (2007), www.jceps.com.

> The deadly banalities of the management consultant and the technocratic expert are universally deployed to justify arbitrary closure, redundancy, the dereliction of building (plant, as they say), as well as the gross, philistine and self-seeing foreshortening of a humane education. We all of us have innumerable such stories to tell. But through it all, with unshakeable self-satisfaction, the managerialists pursue their unimpeded way, entitling new courses 'the management of contractions', 'the organisation of decline', or most risible of all, 'falling rolls'. The inanity of the disciplinary diction should have been enough to kill it off. Stuck with the latter-day and pretentious account of the policy sciences as being capable of bringing about rational progress and the accurate predictions which would permit this consummation, no senior manager ever has recourse to such traditional concepts such as wisdom, sagacity, utter accident, sainthood, passion, tragedy, historical understanding.[20]

Ironically much of the modern policy interventions are not evidence based but are based on belief systems such as the role of private capital in public provision[21] and the need for a flexible, compliant and deployable workforce.[22] Reform is being enabled by policy entrepreneurs who are made up of New Labour ministers and civil servants together with private-sector consultants and advisors who are selected and are brought from schools and the universities to work in Whitehall or non-departmental public bodies such as the NCSL.[23] The attempted seduction of those who are contracted as elite adults through the empowerment of distributed leadership is a fabrication that, as Hartley states, is about tactics and not strategy.[24] The denial of history for and about the child on whom elite adults must impact and gather data from is a form of tyranny that many are complicit in and we should be ashamed.

Problematising history

New Labour policy strategy as 'deliverology' is presented as a new but logically commonsense model where scientific knowledge claims of the school and system as a machine where cause and effect are close together is accepted. Other ideas and debates are seen as disruptive, where people are automatically destroyers who must be neutralised. If there is to be debate then it can only be about localised implementation, it can be about pace and how best things might be done, but not about the substance where the reforms are non-negotiable.[25] So while the rhetoric is about a new improved approach the endemic preference for rationality, hierarchy, and scientific proofs bleeds through. However, and somewhat ironically, in spite of all the hard work of those involved, the limitations of laboratory knowledge claims within social settings remain a problem for deliverers. This is because while human beings are being controlled by contract compliance, performance-related pay and old-fashioned fear of getting things wrong and being named, shamed and sacked in public, it is the case that in the end human beings have to act, and they do this in ways that can be flawed. So the clarity of the picture of deliverology always fades and links in the delivery chain weaken and break because it has within it the causes of its own failure:

---

[20]Fred Inglis, *The Management of Ignorance* (Oxford: Basil Blackwell, 1985), 105–6.
[21]See Stephen J. Ball, *Education PLC* (London: Routledge, 2007).
[22]See Butt and Gunter, *Modernizing Schools*.
[23]Helen M. Gunter and Gillian Forrester, 'New Labour Education Policy and the Rise of School Leadership in England' (paper presented at the American Educational Research Association Annual Meeting, Chicago, April, 2007).
[24]David Hartley, 'The Emergence of Distributed Leadership', *British Journal of Educational Studies* 55, no. 2 (2007): 202–14.
[25]See Peter Hyman, *1 out of 10: From Downing Street Vision to Classroom Reality* (London: Vintage, 2005).

humans make decisions with the best of intentions which may or may not be what was intended by the minister.

Such arguments are not new, and have been a recurring theme in my own work along with colleagues from policy studies.[26] There is a crisis in knowledge production. While the field is pluralistic in relation to knowledge, ways of knowing and range of knowers from practice, policy and higher education, public policy is based on a narrow form of evaluative and instrumental approach to evidence glossed over by belief statements about required behaviours and skills, promoted by a small group of advisors and consultants who work at all levels of government to deliver on targets.[27] Hence I would argue that educational administration needs to engage with some problem posing about scholarship and research:

- Control: policy entrepreneurs determining what the field is, what is to be known and how it is to be known.
- Purposes of scholarship: the role of public intellectual is not understood or recognised as a central identity for field members.
- Purposes of field membership: a lack of ongoing reflection on field purposes and knowledge claims in relation to knowledge production and boundary setting.
- Reading: a lack of respect for the literatures, where there is often narrow reading and citation. It seems that as long as certain 'famous' people are cited then this is all that is needed to demonstrate the relevance of the paper.
- Knowledge claims: a lack of respect for the range of methodologies available in empirical work, and the productive possibilities for research design. Too many projects are determined by commissioners of evaluations rather than designed by researchers in order to undertake scholarly investigations of important questions for and about practice.
- Conceptual frameworks: a lack of respect for disciplinary resources that can be used from the arts, humanities, and social sciences, and while the language is often used (e.g. discourse, field) there is little evidence of reading the original sources and building conceptual explanatory frameworks.
- Field membership: a lack of people in higher education institutions to do the job of scholarship and to work within a diverse field with other field members in developing research.

The current state of the field means that other forms of knowledge (philosophical, experiential, ideological), other ways of knowing (conceptualisations from sociology, history,

[26]I have raised these matters elsewhere. For example, Helen M. Gunter, 'Knowledge Production in the Field of Educational Leadership: A Place for Intellectual Histories', in 'Administration and Leadership in Education: A Case for History', ed. Peter Ribbins, special issue, *Journal of Educational Administration and History* 38, no. 2 (2006): 210–15; Helen M. Gunter, 'Conceptualising Research in Educational Leadership', in 'Researching Leadership – A Review of Progress', special issue, *Educational Management, Administration and Leadership* 33, no. 2 (2005): 165–80; Helen M. Gunter, 'An Analysis of How the Past and Future Are Conceptualised and Used Within the Field of Education Management', *Leading and Managing* 7, no. 1 (2002): 1–14. I am not alone in raising this issue, as Peter Ribbins' special issue of the *Journal of Educational Administration and History* (2006) shows, there are concerns by scholars from around the world and these are included in the special issue: Jill Blackmore, 'Social Justice and the Study and Practice of Leadership in Education: A Historical Perspective', 185–200; Fenwick English, 'Understanding Leadership in Education: Life Writing and its Possibilities', 141–54; Eugiene Samier, 'Educational Administration as a Historical Discipline: An *Apologia Pro Vita Historia*', 125–40.

[27]Helen M. Gunter, 'Conceptualising Research'.

economics, political science, biographies/autobiographies, activist statements about social justice), and other knowers (children, teachers, local authority personnel, headteachers, professors, researchers) can be marginalised and often ridiculed. Importantly, historical work is sidelined because it is epistemologically inconsistent with the type of measurement studies and the instrumental nature of what works that is currently in play. Indeed, I draw inspiration from Samier, who states:

> I see history, like other liberal arts, advocating both a critical perspective and a set of values appropriate for an exploration of the human condition wherever one finds it, including the administrative world. Positivistic and structural-functional approaches to administration are simply not equipped to deal with questions of freedom, authenticity, responsibility and individual action. An understanding of the human condition is not only submerged in organisational levels of analysis, but is suppressed by the very assumptions and methods employed in constructing large scale theories about human behaviour, efficient organisational design and effective management techniques, and is obscured in the current fad of 'leadership training'. They gloss over complexities in the human character, power and politics, ethics in organisational life, and opposed contextual forces shaping the world and mentality of the administrator. Those values and concerns central to humanism – from humanity's greatest aspirations and creative accomplishments to its most fundamental flaws, weaknesses and heinous deeds – consequently find little place for systematic study.[28]

What seems to be at the heart of the problem is the border between the practice of educational administration, which is an example of what Young identifies as the *political* form of knowledge, and disciplinary knowledge, which he calls *theoretical* debates. He argues that the two are distinctive in terms of knowledge claims, where boundaries can be crossed but not erased. It seems that educational administration is dominated by political forms of knowledge focused on the immediacy of problem solving. What is to be done is based on what seems to make sense at that moment in time, and the use of relabelling enables change to be legitimated as modern and new. Consequently, researchers find it difficult to keep 'their autonomy to develop theories which may not be attractive to policymakers'.[29] Theoretical work based on disciplinary knowledge production through methodology and conceptual models is different to political work, and requires researchers to engage in projects and thinking that is necessary but may not be politically acceptable. Historical work became marginalised as researchers located themselves politically as a part of the delivery chain, and a struggle to produce the right theory has developed, and is impossible given Samier's analysis that educational administration needs a humanistic and not scientific rationality.

Historical work and educational administration

One of the jobs that historical work can do is to challenge how modernisation can distort events and help with reconstruction by acknowledging that research is taking place in socially unjust settings.[30] It seems that like Al Gore[31] has recently said in relation to Bush's foreign policy there are some 'convenient untruths' that have to be opened up and analysed. Certainly there is a need to examine the exercise of power and the way that power operates to generate advantage and disadvantage. Through historical work field members can recapture criticality as a means of examining what has happened, what is

[28] Samier, 'Educational Administration', 126.
[29] Michael D. Young, *Bringing Knowledge Back In* (London: Routledge, 2008), 117.
[30] Patti Lather, 'Research as Praxis', *Harvard Educational Review* 56, no, 3 (1986): 257–77.
[31] Al Gore, *The Assault on Reason* (London: Bloomsbury, 2007).

happening and what might happen, and WHY. Criticality has been positioned as oppositional by those involved in delivering change and it has been very easy to do this. Apple draws attention to why neo-liberalism has been so popular and seductive for practitioners and many researchers, not least that it can be used to speak to everyday concerns and issues. Consequently, neo-liberals (in the new right and New Labour) have 'reshaped the common sense of society' and have 'established new identities'.[32] There is much that I have talked about in this article that will not be understood, recognised or given the time of day, and there are many who have a professional and financial stake in the neo-liberal agenda, even if they do not necessarily believe it.

Taking inspiration from Apple we might want to think and take action about how we can speak to the everyday concerns of people, and ask: is this a problem or a fabricated one? What are the real problems in our communities? How might we, in Bates' terms, work on how we might live together and so create identities that are about dialogue and democratic praxis?[33] In recapturing the legitimacy of criticality we can show how knowledge production links to democracy, and what I am increasingly calling productive pluralism.[34] Here the range of knowledge claims, ways of knowing and knowers are respected and given recognition through research as scholarly practice. This does not mean a position cannot be taken, but it must be based on making a case about what is distinctive about this position in relation to others, rather than assuming that others do not exist or are irrelevant or are trouble makers.

Historical work is about the past and the future, but what is important about such scholarship is the lack of certainty, something which deliverology cannot cope with. Silver encapsulates how 'historians trade interpretations' and,

> ...history is also substantively about the future, in ways of which historians are not likely to normally be aware in the act of doing history. The ways in which historical material is ordered, the messages it is induced to carry, tell us not only how the historian perceives a reality but how it is possible to perceive it. The processes point towards a somewhere, towards choices.[35]

The very production of choices in ways that are not just about the market is key to our scholarship, because alternatives in the past and future (what ifs) can be used to understand and legitimate options (can dos). Historical work is not neutral, it requires a sense of reflexivity and positioning that are necessary for democratic approaches to thrive, and it requires a dialogic disposition that both values and engages with ideas. The delivery of change is better informed and owned as a result of research informed by a range of knowledge claims.

However, without historical analysis (which does require an engagement with method and conceptualisation) we remain, in Silver's terms 'busy but blind'.[36] Deliverology has kept us all busy, there have been some local gains as a result, but treating social settings as a laboratory has done damage to the nature of the public, the fabric of our public institutions and the people (including children) who work within public services. While human beings are the central concern of much that policy and research texts talk about, what is said often

---

[32]Michael W. Apple, 'Interrupting the Right: On Doing Critical Educational Work in Conservative Times', in *Education Research in the Public Interest*, ed. Gloria Ladson-Billings and William F. Tate (New York: Teacher's College Press, 2006), 28.

[33]Richard Bates, 'Can We Live Together? The Ethics of Leadership in the Learning Community' (paper presented at the BELMAS annual conference, Milton Keynes, UK, October, 2003).

[34]Helen M. Gunter and Tanya Fitzgerald, 'Educational Administration and History: Debating the Agenda', *Journal of Educational Administration and History* 40, no. 1 (2008): 5–20.

[35]Silver, *Education, Change and the Policy Process*, 7.

[36]Ibid., 245.

fails to grasp the contextual nature of how agency interplays with structures such as place and time. What is missing is what Ozga identifies as the bigger picture, or the ways in which what is happening locally interplays with systemic changes, and how the bigger picture is read and engaged with differently based on embedded cultures and histories.[37]

It seems to me that what we might usefully put on to our agenda are histories 'of' and 'for'. I link the two together as I would not wish there to be a binary separation, as both interplay with the other. Essentially, the types of work that can be 'of' are projects that examine people, institutions, systems and theories/conceptual work. There is work with heads (see work by Gronn, Ribbins, Thomson[38]), examples of schools at work (see work by Ball on *Beachside Comprehensive*, and Elizabeth Richardson's account of *The Teacher, the School and the Task of Management*[39]), education systems over time (see work by Clyde Chitty and Michael Fielding[40]), and theories (a range of work here, and see work by Ball on Foucault, and by Thomson on Bourdieu[41]). Underpinning this are studies of the state and the relationship with the economy, and this requires radical thinking about the role and operation of markets in the provision of public services.[42] What might usefully take place are examinations of policy texts, for example, there is research evidence that challenges the claims made in *teachers: meeting the challenge of change*[43] about the failure of teacher appraisal, and we need histories to be written which show that performance management is premised on a cynical approach to human nature and fabricated evidence.[44] There is much to be done in relation to National Standards, not least the requirement that the job of a headteacher is to implement reform needs to be examined and problematised.[45] We need more ethnographies of schools; more biographies of individuals and networks; we need measurement studies that go back to examine the statistics about the education over time, not least changes to the school workforce. Claims about 'national', 'performance', 'networks', 'world class', 'standards' all need to be problematised.

The writing of a decade of New Labour should not be left to the political scientists, but instead we need in-depth analysis of education policy. Who will write an English version of Callahan's study of the *Cult of Efficiency*[46] about the penetration of the private sector into

[37]Jenny Ozga, 'Modernizing the Education Workforce: A Perspective from Scotland', *Educational Review* 57, no. 2 (2005): 207–19.
[38]Peter Gronn, *The New Work of Educational Leaders* (London: Sage, 2003); Peter Ribbins, ed., *Leaders and Leadership in the School, College and University* (London: Cassell, 1997); Pat Thomson, 'Severed Heads and Compliant Bodies?: A Speculation about Principal Identities', *Discourse* 25, no. 1 (2004): 43–60.
[39]Stephen J. Ball, *Beachside Comprehensive* (Cambridge: Cambridge University Press, 1981); Elizabeth Richardson, *The Teacher, the School and the Task of Management* (London: Heinemann, 1973).
[40]Clyde Chitty, *Education Policy in Britain* (Basingstoke, UK: Palgrave Macmillan, 2004); Michael Fielding, ed., *Taking Education Really Seriously* (London: RoutledgeFalmer, 2001).
[41]Stephen J. Ball, *Foucault and Education* (London: Routledge, 1990); Pat Thomson, 'Bringing Bourdieu to Policy Sociology: Codification, Misrecognition and Exchange Value in the UK context', *Journal of Education Policy* 20, no. 6 (2005): 741–58.
[42]See in particular Roger Dale, *The State and Education Policy* (Milton Keynes, UK: Open University Press, 1989); Ball, *Education PLC.*
[43]Department for Education and Employment (DfEE), *teachers: meeting the challenge of change* (London: DfEE, 1998).
[44]See Helen M. Gunter, 'Teacher Appraisal Research Networks 1980–2000', *Educational Review* 53, no. 3 (2001): 241–50.
[45]Department for Education and Skills, *National Standards for Headteachers*.
[46]Raymond E. Callahan, *Education and the Cult of Efficiency* (Chicago: University of Chicago Press, 1962).

the US public education system? Who will collect the stories of a modernised workforce and produce an English version of Bourdieu et al.'s *Weight of the World*?[47] As I read current articles in newspapers, and I do empirical work in schools, I keep hearing people say that the college or academy is 'free from local authority control'[48] as if this is new or necessary. Schools are not under local authority control but central government control through deliverology, and so the question is who will write the history of curriculum and performance control since the 1944 Act and what will be said about the pre-1988 period when *all* schools had freedom from central government control? We also need to rethink our assumptions and position as researchers, and think otherwise about field purposes. This is particularly important in relation to the place of children in research, and how they tend to be the objects rather than subjects of policy and much evaluative research.[49]

Interplayed with 'of' are histories 'for' and how historical studies of people, processes, practices and institutions can have things to say about current and future practices, conceptualisations, thinking and actions. For example, we need case studies of school, but more importantly, educational improvements that are based on local and professional conceptualisations, where context is involved, but where educational aspirations can be used to shape and structure development.[50] We need to engage with current developments and examine the motivations and consequences of this for practice, e.g. what it means to do remodelling when a headteacher does not agree[51] and how people in real time action have to handle contradictions in policy (the delivery chain is not neat and tidy), and how they have to handle the violence that some policies do to teaching and learning. We can usefully do histories for our own work in relation to programme development and projects that we are interested in, and the types of relationships we construct with a range of funders.

In engaging with historical work we need to remember: first, it is not just about method but is about conceptualisations; second, it is not about narrating events but looking at the shaping and structuring of those events in time and place; third, it requires data collection based on an analysis of documents such as diaries, letters, policy texts, all of which are absent from much work in the field; fourth, it requires criticality so that advantage and disadvantage over time can be revealed and examined; and fifth, action needs to be product of dialogue and strategising. Ultimately, we need to examine the exercise of power and we need to be able to explain this in ways that do not stereotype or essentialise. We need to address issues of social class, race, and gender, and we cannot escape the legacy of colonialism. The field can draw on a range of social theorists to do this, not least Bourdieu's thinking tools of habitus and field,[52] Foucault's theories of discourse and governmentality,[53] and Habermas' theories of communicative action.[54]

---

[47]Pierre Bourdieu et al., *The Weight of World* (Cambridge: Polity Press, 1999).
[48]See the account of Thomas Deacon Academy in A. Asthana, 'No Beak, No Bells in School of the Future', *The Observer*, August 26, 2007, 15.
[49]See Helen M. Gunter and Pat Thomson, 'But, Where Are the Children?', *Management in Education* 21, no. 2 (2007): 23–8.
[50]See Kevin Hollins, Helen M. Gunter, and Pat Thomson, 'Living Improvement: A Case Study of a Secondary School in England', *Improving Schools* 9, no. 2 (2006): 141–52.
[51]See Patrick Yarker, 'On Not Being a Teacher: The Professional and Personal Costs of Workforce Remodelling', *Forum* 47, nos. 2–3 (2005): 169–74.
[52]See Helen M. Gunter, *Leaders and Leadership in Education* (London: PCP, 2001); Pat Thomson, 'Bringing Bourdieu to Policy Sociology'.
[53]See Ball, *Foucault and Education*.
[54]See Rob Smith, 'Work, Identity and the Quasi-market: The FE Experience' (PhD thesis, University of Birmingham, 2004).

Summary

The field needs to recognise the inherited knowledge claims in which it is located, and the imperative is to develop a defendable model of its purposes and practices. Taking Adam's metaphor a stage further, we need to invest in a new canvas. This can emerge by an ongoing dialogue about the nature of the field and debate about knowledge claims. Central to this is how the field has a clear sense of itself and what scholarship means in practice. We need, like Ribbins does, to open up our personal intellectual journeys and how over time there have been struggles with identity and research orientation.[55] My argument is that field members, particularly in higher education and local authorities, and in many schools, have been positioned as irrelevant unless they are captured by the delivery chain and sign up to the deliverology disposition. Many hide away, particularly in schools where there is an attempt to keep off the radar and get on with a professionally determined agenda. Developing scholarship through research design and conceptual frameworks drawn from the humanities and social sciences is one way in which field members can escape the trap of not being a real practitioner or a real academic. Scholarship speaks to practice and the academy, and we are in a unique, privileged and obvious position to do something about it.

Acknowledgements

The reading and thinking that generated this paper is a product of the ESRC-funded Knowledge Production in Educational Leadership Project (RES-000-23-1192). I would like to thank the ESRC for the funding and Dr Gillian Forrester for her scholarship and commitment.

[55]Peter Ribbins, 'History and the Study of Administration and Leadership in Education: Introduction to a Special Issue', *Journal of Educational Administration and History* 38, no. 2 (2006): 113–24.

The state of Denmark

Peter Gronn

When an editor sanctions a set of authors to expound on what they believe is blighting the world of education, who can be sure of what they are likely to suggest? Not surprisingly, in the present instance the authors of the six papers in this collection have seized on the freedom they have been granted and have outlined a range of afflictions. The potential of such an open agenda is to make the job of discussant a hazardous one. If, however, there turn out to be points of connection between the issues that are keeping the authors awake at night, or even evidence of overlap in their concerns, then a discussant's search for thematic coherence is made slightly easier. As I hope to show, there are occasions when their arguments have converged and others when they have diverged. There are also, it should be said, points they make that need to be contested and do not necessarily go without saying. But overall, their collective assessment is reminiscent of Hamlet's verdict on the ailing state of the kingdom at Elsinore: there are things that are rotten in the realm of school leadership. Broadly speaking, three of the contributions are concerned primarily about policy and what the authors (Fitzgerald, Wrigley and Gunter) see as its potential to corrupt forms of professional practice, two (Wilkinson, and Bates and Eacott) have scholars in their sights either for what they have said or have left unsaid, while one (Thomson) rather neatly bridges these two sets of concerns by highlighting features of practice neglected by scholars with a view to stimulating their possible future engagement. It is roughly on the basis of this three-fold differentiation that I have structured my commentary, although from time to time as will be evident I have dipped in and out of particular papers at will. I begin with the issues raised by Pat Thomson.

The school wars

When human beings are not tearing themselves apart in wars over guns and butter and cold wars, not to mention the war on terror, they generally have surrogate forms of warfare available for sublimating their aggressive instincts. Those of us with memories that stretch back far enough, for example, will be able to recall the paradigm wars (alluded to briefly by Terry Wrigley). These occurred when, in the wake of an unrelenting assault on the edifice of science and a monolithic scientific worldview, scholars from across the social sciences began bunkering down as card-carrying adherents of various theories and attacked their opponents in an effort to discredit them on a range of epistemological, ontological or methodological grounds. Then, in Australia at least, the culture wars and, within the framework of their larger compass, the history wars, have held public stage for the last decade and a half. As an expatriate Australian watching from a distance during 2007, I was astonished by the growing sense of disbelief, foreboding and horror with which self-confessed right-wing journalistic critics (from within the relative safety of their Murdoch press bunkers) viewed the impending collapse of their much favoured Howard government. After 11 years in office, the Coalition finally fell on its sword on the last Saturday in November, when a thumping 5% two-party preferred swing leftwards ejected numerous government members and ministers from the federal parliament and, most insulting and humiliating of all, inflicted political death on the Prime Minister himself when, after more than 30 years representation, he lost his own parliamentary seat. In short, the Right was belted. Its initial bewildered response was to lurch alternatively between lament at the prospect of leftish cultural revival[1] and re-assurance that Howard's cultural war legacy was sufficiently robust to withstand attempted dismantling by so-called 'Howard-haters'.[2]

But there is another war. And for those of us in education, this is a much more serious and important war. À la *Fawlty Towers*, it is also one of those wars that should not be mentioned or named as such because it is called the war on schools. This is my designation, I hasten to add, and not one adopted by any of these authors although they provide plenty of supporting evidence for what I have in mind. An inherent feature of schooling and schools is that there is rarely a time when they are not battlegrounds: interest groups press their claims about what should go on in classrooms, reformers peddle their pet projects, theorists mount their critiques and, when it suits them, politicians and authorities occasionally and unpredictably ambush practitioners. Significantly, however, the ante is upped considerably when the state's strategy hardens into one of rounding on its own schools, especially the people in charge of them, not merely by means of the compliance afforded by a vast regime of audit and surveillance, but as an English cabinet minister did recently with calculated assaults on head teachers and governors over alleged breaches of student admission codes. Indeed, such resort to public humiliation and demonisation (akin, perhaps, to dunking witches or locking suspected miscreants in the stocks in a town square and pelting them with fruit) has now become a weapon of first resort in this war. Indeed, so far have the rules of engagement shifted that government spokespersons often combine forces with the media to chase down instances of feral leadership in order to publicly purge them. Is it any wonder that such experiences spawn a culture of complaint and lament among heads' and principals' associations – neatly captured in a respondent's words in a recent survey by three Australian secondary principal peak bodies: 'I do love my job but it is killing me. I cannot sleep and [am] feeling really unwell'.[3] Needless to say, as is implied by this choice of wording, if this is as good as this new form of media blood sport gets for school heads, then, like Pat Thomson, one wonders why the National Association of Headteachers (NAHT) has even bothered to re-enter a social partnership with the UK government.

Head banging and kicking heads

As I write this commentary, the proceedings of the NAHT's annual conference have just concluded in Liverpool. The NAHT's website is loaded with conference documents

[1]See G. Sheridan, 'Howard's Grand Failure', *Australian*, October 25, 2007; G. Sheridan, 'Liberal Future Lies in Tony Abbott's Ideas', *Australian*, November 22, 2007.
[2]J. Albrechtson, 'Under Labor, Elites Remain Irrelevant', *Australian*, February 27, 2008; J. Albrechtson, 'Paul, You've Missed the Point and Lost the Plot', *Australian*, February 29, 2008.
[3]National Secondary Principals' Associations, 'Making a Difference … Counting the Cost', National Secondary Principals' Associations' Research Report into School Leader Welfare (2007), http://aspa.asn.au/images/surveys/schoolleadersurveyreport2007at20080214.pdf (accessed May 7, 2008).

concerned with the plight of head teachers. For these reasons, the issues raised in Thomson's paper could not be timelier. Her questions, essentially, are: Should heads resist government policy and should school leadership scholars engage with resistance?

Resistance pre-supposes agency. Some degree of agency is always possible, as 'no monarch or dictator or group of oligarchs is ever absolute'. This is because their rule is 'not only subject to the data of the national situation' but 'also subject to the necessity of acting with some people, of getting along with others, of neutralizing still others and of subduing the rest'.[4] Heads exercise agency and, as Thomson suggests, they have always managed to take care of bureaucracy in the interests of their schools because, as an NAHT survey on the impact of Office for Standards in Education (OfSTED) inspections expresses it, 'context is all'.[5] Thus, in Australia, for example, where merit-based school principal selection processes operate, principals have contrived, when they have deemed it necessary for their school contexts, to secure the appointment of preferred internal applicants for leadership vacancies.[6] But agency, including that of heads, and the autonomy of schools (see below), are constrained, especially when the evidence of target-determined performance ceases to run in a school's favour. The impact of constraints (Thomson's idea of corralling) may begin to crank up a few notches when governments make policy adjustments in light of experiences of weaknesses and flaws or they re-write the rules. In doing so, the ground is laid for a game of cat and mouse, the steps in which are, roughly: discover a context-based work-around or policy loophole > exploit it to your advantage as a practitioner > perhaps diffuse it to other schools or fellow head teachers > hope and pray that auditors or policy wonks do not become wise to it > but then watch helplessly if they try to amend it or replace it with a new procedure > interpret this as yet another incentive to play further avoidance games, and the cycle begins again. For these reasons, target-setting may be susceptible to resistance, as Hood notes that it was by state managers in the former Soviet Union, through versions of 'target gaming'. This is a creative mode of compliance that is accomplished by agencies through such phenomena as ratchet effects (negotiation of undemanding, hard to miss targets), threshold effects (concentration in the provision of services on agency clients marginally close to cut-off bands in order to lift average scores) and output distortions (disallowance of appointment bookings more than 48 hours in advance to ensure that consultations occur within a 48-hour target range).[7]

Part of the reason why the kind of *de facto* collusion between media and government school warriors adverted to earlier occurs, is that the school wars are now being fought by global players, on a global scale and in global theatres (e.g. Programme for International Student Assessment (PISA) and Progress in International Reading Literacy Study (PIRLS)). By electing to make their school systems hostages to fortune in a battle royal between international comparators, governments have chosen to lock themselves into an arranged marriage strategy for the delivery of desired outcomes: a horse and cart hybrid of degrees of site-based autonomy and performance-based measures of accountability. A recent European Commission report on the making of site-level decisions about funding and

[4]J.A. Schumpeter, *Capitalism, Socialism and Democracy*, 6th ed. (1943; repr., London: Counterpoint/Unwin, 1987), 245.
[5]National Association of Headteachers, 'Ofsted Style Inspections Contribute to Poor Retention', http://www.naht.org.uk/themes/campaign-item-view.asp?ID=3885&sid=28 (accessed May 6, 2008).
[6]P. Gronn and K. Lacey, 'Cloning Their Own: Aspirant Principals and the School-based Selection Game', *Australian Journal of Education* 50, no. 2 (2006): 102–22.
[7]C. Hood, 'Gaming in Targetworld: The Targets Approach to Managing British Public Services', *Public Administration Review* 66, no. 4 (2007): 517–18.

human resources in 30 countries is apposite on this aspect of the war on schools.[8] Distinguishing between full, partial and implied degrees of school autonomy, the report is unequivocal that the roll out of devolved decision-making from the mid-1980s was determined top-down by centralised legislative enactment:

> Schools themselves did not seek autonomy, the legislation made provision for the transfer of new duties without schools having any right to express their view on the matter. In fact, schools acquired new responsibilities in spite of their own wishes.[9]

In effect, then, the political and policy elites prevailed. Yet, given the unintended negative consequences it generates, this autonomy-accountability thrust (which has been central to New Labour's modernisation agenda) is looking increasingly like a fundamentally flawed strategy. Moreover, considered in light of the following examples, it is perhaps even more extraordinary that the resistance of head teacher associations sought by Thomson has not been stronger.

Off with their heads!

'High stakes' is the normal way of describing accountability pressures. This is partly due to the levels of risk-taking and risk management required by increased school autonomy. Equally, one of the signals communicated by the mantra of leadership in countries such as Scotland is an encouragement to head teachers and school leaders generally to adopt a 'go for it' mentality if their schools are to make a difference. But in such circumstances governments, national and local, still cling to their right to arbitrate on whether or not the risks associated with particular heads' initiatives are acceptable (thereby, ironically, revealing their own risk aversiveness). Government–media collusion in this instance takes the form of heads deemed to be behaving badly being publicly exposed and 'hung out to dry'.

In a recent Scottish example of what I mean, a primary head teacher, with the backing of his school board, tried to tackle the problem of childhood obesity by imposing a ban on children bringing sweets from home with them to school. In effect, the school was trying to create a no-go zone – to communicate the message that for such time as pupils were within its bounds they would not be permitted to eat anything which might be potentially injurious to their health. The understanding was that whenever sweets were brought in, they were confiscated until the end of the day and then returned to the children. Some parents objected. Stared down by these complaints, the local council informed the head that he had no authority to implement the measure and that he should rescind it. The *Guardian* report of this story[10] was accompanied by a photograph of a mother (a solidly built mum it has to be said) with her two wee laddies (one of them decidedly chubby looking) standing outside the school fence and brandishing Kit Kat bars. For the reader, there is a clear message of defiance (even truculence) in this image communicated by the thin-lipped smirks on the three faces. The text of the paper communicates an even stronger tone of: 'Who do these people (head teacher and board) think they are? How dare they!' The moral of the story for head teachers (and, more importantly, prospective heads) is surely something like: 'Stick your head above the parapet and you will be dealt with unmercifully. Do not expect support from your employer who instead will not only name, blame and shame you for your folly, but will also undermine

[8] European Commission, 'School Autonomy in Europe: Policies and Measures' (Brussels: Eurydice, European Unit, 2007), http://www.eurydice.org (accessed May 1, 2008).
[9] Ibid., 15.
[10] J. Kemp, 'Battle of a Wee Laddie's Twix', *Guardian*, March 27, 2007.

your future authority'. Here, then, is a perfect illustration of how heads become victims of the pincer movement created by the autonomy–accountability interplay.

But it gets worse. There can be no doubt that headship has become a blood sport, as in these next examples of governments and media colluding in support of (some) parents:

- A Scottish secondary head teacher who had allowed students to sit their Standard Grade exams in S3 rather than S4, was suspended by his local council. This action followed a critical Her Majesty's Inspectorate of Education (HMIE) report that had taken issue with the head's practice on the grounds that there was insufficient time to properly prepare pupils and after HMIE described the school's curriculum as 'weak'. The school in question had dropped its early presentation policy, but HMIE believed the head and the school had still not made sufficient progress in implementing an action plan.[11]
- A Scottish primary head was frog-marched out of her school by local council officers after being suspended, following criticism of her leadership by HMIE, concerns raised in a parental survey and for failing to implement an action plan for improvement.[12]
- A primary school principal in Victoria, Australia, described as 'dependable, loving, unflappable', who had had to deal with a number of traumatic school events early in his principalship (including the death of a pupil and three bodily assaults on himself by parents), and who was working relentlessly for seven days a week at his job, took his own life.[13]
- A Scottish primary head teacher also took her own life. She was upset after being verbally criticised during an HMIE inspection. After this, the local council director of education talked with head teachers, some of whom 'were in tears' because 'they have to keep things "bottled up" and "have to be seen to be leaders but underneath might be in turmoil"'.[14]

Why, it has to be asked, have things reached this point? Is the situation now one, as Helen Gunter suggests, of trial by media, or open season on heads?

The collective voice of defiant heads may offer a way of avoiding these types of tragedies. If in fact they are so fed up with a vast bureaucratic apparatus of compliance, surveillance and media free-for-alls to which they and their schools are in thrall (with the attendant reform fatigue, work intensification, threats to well-being and so on), to what extent might heads' joint interests be furthered by something like the good old-fashioned trade union tactic of working to rule, for example, thereby stalling the reform imperative and the worst excesses of the delivery warriors (see below)? It is not as if head teachers are ignorant of the government's strategy: impose on schools a 'level of accountability designed to raise the game in order to demonstrate to tax-paying voters that they are in firm control of education and can get schools to deliver on their electoral pledges', was how NAHT President Clarissa Williams summarised it to her troops at Liverpool.[15] In short: at all costs endeavour to appease an

[11]A. Denholm, 'Headteacher Who Let Pupils Sit Exams a Year Early Is Suspended', *Glasgow Herald*, March 24, 2007.
[12]A. Denholm, 'Council Officials Escort Head Out of School', *Glasgow Herald*, November 16, 2007.
[13]S. Waldon and J-A. Davies, 'Special Report: Suicide – Men at Risk', *Age*, August 18, 2003.
[14]A. Denholm, 'Call for School Inspectors to Ease Visit Stress after Headteacher's Death', *Glasgow Herald*, May 3, 2008.
[15]National Association of Headteachers, 'President's Annual Conference Speech', http://www.naht.org.uk/themes/campaign-item-view.asp?ID=3885&sid=28 (accessed May 8, 2008).

aspirational, overly agitated and anxious middle class.[16] Thomson quotes the NAHT's Mick Brookes on its endorsement of the social partnership and the commitment to an intensive (weekly) dialogue with the UK government this entails, while in the same breath acknowledging the lack of trust of teachers and heads (Tanya Fitzgerald's concern). When she assembles a list of the NAHT's conference resolutions Pat Thomson is perfectly correct in highlighting their broad alignment with the policy criticisms of researchers and then chastising her researcher peers for taking the voice of head teachers' associations insufficiently seriously. But for all of the effort entailed in adopting such conference resolutions, one is still left wondering about the extent of their overall impact on government policy, which goes to the heart of the issue of whether professional associations are better off trying to position themselves inside the (policy) tent or staying right outside of it altogether.

Cleansing

Helen Gunter, Tanya Fitzgerald and Terry Wrigley focus on the impact of aspects of the public service modernisation agenda in the UK and New Zealand. Tanya Fitzgerald's concern is the erosion of trust in teachers since the late 1980s, grounded in a politics of mistrust and accomplished by a machinery of regulation, compliance and audit, which results in the de-professionalisation of teachers and their pedagogy. Terry Wrigley focuses on 'improvement'. Because he sees this as an ideologically loaded and paradigmatically privileged term, he regards the quest for 'School Improvement' as hegemonic and therefore worthy of critique. Finally, Helen Gunter questions the change narrative that informs New Labour's modernisation policy and the importation of private-sector practices for the provision of services. One of the things that unites the three authors is their desire to cleanse education of these developments, for which they blame either neo-liberalism (Fitzgerald and Wrigley) or a neo-liberal and neo-conservative combination (Gunter). Cleansing, of course, is also a strong part of the impulse which informed New Labour's desire to re-model and streamline the UK public services – to rid these of what it saw as bureaucratic inefficiency and provider (or producer) capture.

Whatever it takes

The key delivery warrior for the Blair government (at least during its second coming between 2001 and 2005) was Michael (later Sir Michael) Barber and his fellow disciples in the Prime Minister's Delivery Unit (PMDU). Barber, the target of Helen Gunter's (and to some extent Terry Wrigley's) wrath, was both architect of and apostle for the gospel of 'deliverology', forged to achieve the outcomes that are part of the Blairites' new covenant with the electorate. Armed with this doctrinal sanction, Barber acted as self-proclaimed prime ministerial 'enforcer'[17] in a regime that, from the author's account of it in his book *Instruction to Deliver*, reads as a version of soft-state Stalinism (albeit without the guns and the Gulags).[18] The quintessence of what it meant to be a delivery warrior under Blair is evident in the

[16] A. Cooper, 'The State of Mind We're In: Social Anxiety, Governance and the Audit Society', *Psychoanalytic Studies* 3, nos. 3–4 (2001): 349–62.

[17] M. Barber, *Instruction to Deliver: Tony Blair, Public Services and the Challenge of Achieving Targets* (London: Politico's Publishing, 2007), 46.

[18] Lest it be thought that the parallel with Stalinism may be drawing too long a bow, witness the author's self-confession that: 'I knew exactly how I needed to behave in John [Gieve]'s meeting – like a Bolshevik commissar after the Russian Revolution, urging greater rigour and more urgency, and rejecting any excuses or backsliding'. Ibid., 156.

opening chapter of Barber's book. Deliverology boils down to a holy trinity of three essential doctrines: engagement, focus and momentum. (With apologies to the first epistle to the Corinthians: And now abide engagement, focus and momentum, these three, and the greatest of these is momentum.) A fellow Blairite warrior, Peter Hyman, claims that momentum is essential for governments otherwise they run the risk of drifting and (worse still?) being seen to drift.[19] Barber's job was to engage the people that needed to be engaged with modernisation targets, to keep them focused and, above all else, to try to sustain the government's overall momentum by maintaining it in a state of siege or permanent revolution.

New Labour deliverology came complete with its own syllabus of errors (in the form of zero tolerance for a hit list of 14 targeted dysfunctional practices in education, health, transport and criminal justice).[20] To be able to deliver required a rather muscular mindset: an amalgam of self-confessed religious moralising, scars inflicted by 1960s student radicalism, exasperation with Militant Tendency labourism and an establishment of breast-beating and hand-wringing liberal wets, visceral loathing of losing (anything), contempt for (perceived) academic procrastination and paralysis, impatience with old buffer Sir Humphrey-style mandarinite bureaucracy, championing of consumer empowerment, advocacy of 'cutting through' at all costs, self-imposition of a frenetic and a punishing work ethic, all of which is marinated with a sense of urgency: in short, a new millennium puritannical fervour.[21] This is a mindset consistent with William James' idea of the twice-born soul,[22] for whom the achievement of healthy-mindedness requires that one make war both on oneself (for the sins of a past life) and on this-worldly naturalism. It is a way of thinking which is obsessive about control and compliance, passionate in its avowal of linear causality and determined to try to root out unintended (or, as Barber terms them, 'perverse') consequences. Equally, deliverology is also other-worldly in its disdain for the idea of human imperfectability, in its indifference towards the well-documented limitations of rationalistic decision-making[23] and in its ignorance of bounded rationality.[24] But above all, in its tone of forced humility and the constant injunctions of its director to PMDU staff to remain humble and avoid complacency at all costs, deliverology functioned as a kind of hyper-rationalistic calculus.

Uncivilising mission?

Barber is unequivocal that if the Prime Minister's track record (note: not that of the government) is to be judged by the statistics assembled by the PDMU, then (perhaps in his ultimate act of humility) 'they do not add up to the transformative change he has promised'.[25] What, then, is the verdict to be on deliverology as an approach to providing publicly funded services? It is worth re-emphasising that Barber's line of report was directly to Tony Blair; that is, to the leader of the party rather than to the cabinet or the government as a whole. It should also be remembered that, historically, as the parties of progress, Western labour and social

---

[19]P. Hyman, *1 out of 10: From Downing Street Vision to Classroom Reality* (London: Vintage, 2005), 384; and see Barber, *Instruction to Deliver*, 211.
[20]Barber, *Instruction to Deliver*, 50.
[21]Ibid., 3–39.
[22]W. James, *The Varieties of Religious Experience* (1901–2; repr., Glasgow: William Collins, 1981), pp. 172, 352.
[23]G. Lakomski, 'Cognition Versus Emotion?: Revising the Rationalist Model of Decision-making' (working paper, 2008), 4.
[24]H.A. Simon, *Administrative Behavior: A Study of Decision-making Processes in Administrative Organization* (1945; repr. New York: Free Press, 1976), xxix and passim.
[25]Barber, *Instruction to Deliver*, 267.

democratic parties have been by their nature reforming and sometimes reconstructionist. Their commitment to the realisation of ideals of human betterment has not infrequently carried with it quasi-religious overtones: creation of a good society or kingdom on Earth of a secular kind, but associated nonetheless with the imagery of a heavenly city or 'New Jerusalem'. For this, in Britain, William Blake's famous poem 'Jerusalem' was a source of inspiration, while in Australia, left-wing true believers often hearken back to post-World War 2 Australia and Prime Minister Ben Chifley's image of the 'light on the hill'. Fast forward to an age of celebrity politics, in which the charismatic Blair brand was the government's key asset, and this link between the PMDU and the Prime Minister probably made a lot of sense, for it identified and projected the leader and his priorities in quasi-religious terms electorally as a kind of saviour who brings results.

Labour governments always live on borrowed time: in the previous millennium, their opponents warmed the leather seats of the Treasury benches for far more electoral cycles than they did in the UK, Australia and New Zealand. Such lengthy periods in waiting tend to breed an impatience to get on with things. Couple this with labour's reconstructionist ideals and its commitment to deliver, and to be seen to have delivered by providing evidence of having done so (particularly when the party and its leader were themselves the victims of a fog of spin for which they were responsible during their first term), then deliverology is perfectly understandable. (Critics might still object, of course, that deliverology represents the acme of spin.) Moreover, the spectre of having long been fingered by its opponents as big spending and profligate with other people's money when in government has always haunted labour parties. Thus, having noble intentions and giving delivery one's best shot were unlikely to be sufficient. For all these reasons and more, a legacy of demonstrable improvement in the lot of significant numbers of British people, particularly its own traditional working-class constituency support base, is what New Labour in office was going to strive for. The slogan adopted by the newly elected Australian government is 'Delivering to working families', while in 2001, New Labour defined its civilising mission as:

> the development of public services of real quality, which citizens from all backgrounds want to use, which deliver quality as well as high standards and which make productive use of every penny of the taxpayers' money which is entrusted to the government.[26]

From its point of view, if accountability and the entire kit and caboodle of performativity targeting would go some way to achieving this end then so be it.

When the logic of justification for delivering is laid out in this way, I find it hard, if I'm honest, not to have some sympathy for it. For this reason, while I would shy from the first part of the second prong in Barber's approach to improving education – 'letting the market rip while protecting equity'[27] – I confess to being more sanguine than Terry Wrigley is about improvement. When I inspect his Figure 1, I can agree with him that a narrowly conceived view of improvement anchored mainly on test results and the subordination of moral and social values to success indicators are suspect, but what is the in-principle objection to adopting some form of evidence of improvement? It ought to be possible to distinguish between assessing pupil progress and the use of test results for league table accountability purposes. Likewise, to try to ensure that the attitudes and practices of civil servants are oriented in the direction of improvement and in the interests of equity seems equally reasonable. For this reason, when I read about Barber's own personal intervention in the life of a 14-year-old

---

[26]Cited in ibid., 232.
[27]Ibid., 207.

boy who was truanting in East London, again I have some sympathy: as the boy had not been expelled, the local council could not offer him a programme; in addition, because the boy's school was across the borough boundary the council claimed it was not responsible for him, but the school said he was no longer on the roll; finally, the council offered him a place on an excluded pupils' scheme, but he did not show up (Why would he? He was a truant); no-one visited his home and no-one checked to see if he had accepted the offer. Later, the lad was arrested for grievous bodily harm. Barber attempted to pressure local authorities into better integrating their data systems on at-risk children and for his sins was accused of trying to be bureaucratic.[28]

Mission impossible?

In the end, who is it that delivers? Peter Hyman left his Downing Street bunker to become a classroom warrior by sampling life at the pointy end at Islington Green School in East London. The experience changed his view on delivery. Echoing my earlier point about the significance of context, Hyman came to the realisation that, at the end of the day, it is heads and teachers and their plans that deliver:

> Government had to hand down policy that applied to 4,000 secondary schools, yet each school was at a different stage of reform, and needed different solutions. Government policy-making simply was not suited to the individual needs of schools, just as politicians believed that schools were not paying enough attention to the individual needs of students. What good heads were doing was to take the policy and implement it at in a way that suited *their* school.[29]

In this connection, Terry Wrigley is right to highlight student poverty and its neglect by School Effectiveness/School Improvement (SESI) warriors. (Thrupp has suggested recently how, through school-level studies of the social geography of school composition – that are sensitive to the important distinction between school-based and school-caused factors influencing student achievement – contextual diversity and the concerns of the SESI community might be brought together to their mutual advantage.[30]) Wrigley is equally right to emphasise that formal qualifications matter to working-class families and minority ethnic students, which to my way of thinking is all the more reason why 'improvement' matters as well. But one of the things that Peter Hyman's time at Islington Green also taught him was that it is equally as important to address fatalism as it is poverty: many of the working-class children and parents he met were still ground down by what Tony Blair called the 'dead weight of low expectations' and lack of self-belief. For Hyman, 'self-belief is the essence of what makes a middle-class person middle class' and he wanted working-class parents to become more pushy like the middle class and demand 'the best for their child'.[31]

The sacrificial lambs for New Labour, as Gunter and Fitzgerald highlight, have been working professionals. (There's a wariness of teachers as self-serving, for example, right throughout Barber's book.) The argument about professional status and autonomy deserves much more space than I can give it here. Teachers in many countries have long sought professional recognition and accountability to their profession, rather than to the state, as Tanya

[28]Ibid., 228–9.
[29]Hyman, *1 out of 10*, 203 (original emphasis).
[30]M.Thrupp, R. Lupton, and C. Brown, 'Pursuing the Contextualisation Agenda: Recent Progress and Future Prospects', in *International Handbook of School Effectiveness and Improvement*, ed. T. Townsend (Dordrecht: Springer, 2007), 111–25.
[31]Hyman, *1 out of 10*, 354 (all quotes).

Fitzgerald suggests. Part of the difficulty in this regard lies in deciding what counts as the profession and then determining who is to speak on its behalf. Sometimes, for example, head teachers are guilty of referring to themselves exclusively as 'the profession'; at others they include their teacher colleagues. Can teacher unions be the voice of the teaching profession? Perhaps, but the objection to that suggestion usually is that unions are primarily industrial bodies concerned with pay and conditions. Then there's the recent history of the professions in England where the report card, in all honesty, is somewhat mixed. Harold Perkin's book *The Rise of Professional Society* indicates that attempts by occupational groups to acquire the kind of autonomy and status traditionally enjoyed by doctors and lawyers has often turned out to be a claim to monopoly status.[32] A strong strand of anti-professional opinion has existed in England that is consistent with the suggestion (attributable to the playwright and author George Bernard Shaw) that the professions are a conspiracy against lay people. For these reasons there's a dilemma: while teachers are not deserving of the kind of shabby and demeaning treatment governments often mete out to them (which betrays an acute lack of trust), to be able to win the argument that they (or any other 'service' or 'care' groups aspiring to professional status, for that matter) deserve autonomy in the definition, control and monitoring of their work, they will need to show that this is not a claim for privilege.

Counter reformation

If there is still a fight to be carried forward in school leadership, and a battle to be won, then the final two papers in this set, by Jane Wilkinson, and Richard Bates and Scott Eacott, address issues concerned with how this should be resourced. Their discussion (and the last part of Helen Gunter's) boils down to the question of just how robust the conceptual tools are with which they and their peers within the field are working.

Fast knowledge

Bates and Scott describe the provision of preparation programmes for school leaders in Australia. As someone who, with Richard Bates, was a participant in the take-off and expansion phases of university-based Masters degree programmes in school leadership over the last three decades or so, I find their conclusions, frankly, dispiriting. First of all, on the basis of a largish sample, they identify what can only be described as a bewildering overall pattern of provision. On the credit side of the ledger, an examination of course reading lists suggests that textbooks have largely been abandoned (thank goodness), that the authorship and content of texts and readings have been de-Americanised and that the spread of authors is increasingly Antipodean as well as Anglo-American. On the debit side (for me, at any rate), the dominance of the theme of change is a genuine surprise, although if I think about it, it should not be. After all, 'change' – which, although much used, is devoid of any particular concrete referent or context and is simply something 'out there' – is emblematic of what has become an era of fast knowledge, in which students, increasingly heavily reliant on the Internet need not even visit libraries (let alone know where to locate one on a campus) and can engage minimally with knowledge defined in the traditional discipline sense.

If I sound nostalgic, then I am, deliberately so. This homogenisation around a rather vacuous concept of change tells us something about what markets do to knowledge: they reduce it to a lowest common denominator. There is a stark contrast between what Bates

[32]H. Perkin, *The Rise of Professional Society: England since 1880* (London: Routledge, 1990), 472–519.

and Eacott now describe and the situation in Australia, certainly in the state of Victoria, as recently as 10–15 years ago. This is because if a prospective post-graduate student aspired to be a school leader during much of the 1980s and well into the 1990s, and wanted to enrol in an Education Faculty programme, she or he had a varied array of options from which to choose to enrol. If that student lived in Melbourne, for example, and wanted to savour the Frankfurt School at Waurn Ponds, then s/he headed south-west to Deakin University. If, by contrast, the student wanted a very small 'L' liberal-soft cuddly diet with a dash of cultural Marxism, then s/he went to the south-east of the city to Monash University. On the other hand, if a heavily inner urban-oriented 'engage with the working class'-style programme was desired, then that same student probably went to the northern suburbs to Latrobe University. Finally, if the preference was for something on more conventional and mainstream lines, then it would probably have been satisfied at the University of Melbourne. In short, there was a smorgasbord of offerings. Now, nearly two decades later, such variety and diversity have all but disappeared, which is sad, because in their own unique ways colleagues at all four locations were engaged in innovative, imaginative, distinctive and intellectually challenging work.

Local, global or 'glocal' knowledge?

Bates' and Eacott's paper also has something to say about how knowledge travels. They show that the reference points from which Australian scholars define their compass or take their bearings are increasingly home-grown. But there is an irony here because, while the source of diffusing theories and knowledge during the early period was mainly the USA – which Helen Gunter also touched on in her opening mention of the theory movement – the recent 'Australianisation' has occurred at a time when the pressures conducive to emerging globalised knowledge communities have increased. In one way, then, is there any purpose served by having knowledge firewalled within national boundaries? On the other hand, as a vice-chancellor or university president you might want to be able to play the (institutional and) nationalist card, if I may put it that way, if you are concerned about global rankings and are keen to trumpet the performance of national research 'stars'. Given also that there are still strongly differentiated national (and sub-national) approaches to leadership policy and practice (as between Scotland and England, for example), then student awareness of home-grown knowledge that addresses problems in home-grown contexts remains a priority.

Diverse knowledge and past knowledge?

What about those who profess the knowledge just described? Sadly, here too, as Jane Wilkinson demonstrates, there is persistent evidence of homogeneity: white, anglo-Celtic middle-class, male assumptions still dominate scholarly writings in the field. To this extent, the privilege about which I have just cautioned in relation to the professions applies with equal force in this area. Moreover, this domain is another example, following the earlier example of the PMDU, of where, in Wilkinson's view, good intentions are not enough and evidence of delivery would be welcome (although, in fairness, she does not express it in this way). And again, as with Terry Wrigley's paper, Jane Wilkinson indicates how our language for capturing reality frequently lets us down to the cost of some people – here women and those minorities that represent ethnic diversity and difference.

An important issue that arises out of Wilkinson's discussion concerns 'othering'. Writing as a white, ageing, middle-class, straight and married male probably disqualifies me from saying anything credible about this, except that I think othering works in two ways. To the extent that being able to tick all of the boxes on the criteria just listed continues to represent a pathway to privilege and power, then those who do not fit that kind of profile are right to feel that they are being othered. The flipside of this, however, is that the person who is able to tick most or all the boxes is made to feel at best guilty and at worst a victim. In short, if these ticks count as strikes against someone, then that someone becomes, in effect, an endangered species and likely to be othered out of existence by virtue of not being PC. With respect to gender, there is no magic bullet for altering the mobilisation of bias in favour of males (otherwise it would likely have been found by now) and so it is necessary to keep on chipping away. Of Wilkinson's two solutions, the ethnicity and gender audit is by far the more promising, in my view, although her second suggestion about self-awareness of representation is still helpful. Every now and then the texture of the landscape does change. Taking just two spheres as illustrations, government and organised religion, if I compare Australia in early 2008 with late 2007, the deputy Prime Minister and deputy Leader of the Opposition are now both women, the Governor General is a woman and the Anglican Church, for the first time in its history, has two women bishops. Small numbers, perhaps, but impressive (and significant) examples – although still all Anglo-Celtic.

In the fight-back, or counter-reformation as I have termed it, as a possible antidote to the ills documented in these papers, Helen Gunter proposes a role for history. But we need to be clear that there are dangers with history, as the late David Halberstam has so eloquently reminded us, for it lends itself to distortion by the 'history boys': persons with vested interests who actively re-write history to further those interests. Those who know better, those who really know their history best, says Halberstam, 'tend to be tempered by it':

> They rarely refer to it so sweepingly and with such confidence. They know that it is the most mischievous of mistresses and that it touts sure things about as regularly as the tip sheets at the local track. Its most important lessons sometimes come cloaked in bitter irony. By no means does it march in a straight line toward the desired result, and the good guys do not always win.[33]

Deliverologists march in straight lines towards desired policy results and, for them, much of the past is anathema: in Michael Barber's case, the educational 1970s was, indeed, another country. What is more, he is also a student of history. Whether historical accounts of such things as policy texts and performance management can be used to set the record (let alone to set it straight), as Gunter proposes, is a moot point. And to let history be the judge is to wait until the dust falls. The problem is that it rarely does, at least not for long enough.

Conclusion

I have been concerned in this commentary to address the implications of some of the major concerns raised in this set of six papers. Necessarily, I had had to be selective, but without, I hope, being (unduly) arbitrary. Some items, such as Tanya Fitzgerald's concern about the managerial gaze and surveillance more generally (given that there are an estimated 4.2 million surveillance cameras in Britain), deserved more of an airing than they received. Standards did not get a run either and, as with surveillance, the range of issues here adds up a huge topic in its own right. Equally, however, there were other discussion possibilities not raised by the authors. No-one, for example, suggested the abolition of school inspection regimes as a way of easing the accountability pressures on teachers (even the NAHT

[33] D. Halberstam, 'The History Boys', *Vanity Fair*, June 2007, 122–6, http://www.vanityfair.com/politics/features/2007/08/halberstam200708

endorses inspection). This is curious as inspection has been abolished in Victoria for 25 years and no government, of whatever political complexion, has been willing to re-introduce it and, to the best of my knowledge, there is no school inspection in the USA. Little point is served, however, by speculating about other gaps, absences and possibilities in the discussion. In conclusion, and bearing in mind these few caveats, this set of papers has hopefully succeeded in saying something insightful and useful about the current state of play in the kingdom of school leadership.

INDEX